TWENTIETH CENTURY SERIES

PROPHET OF SOCIAL INJUSTICE

An Exposition of Amos

By

FREDK. A. TATFORD

HAROLD H. WASSON

G. Allen Fleece Library
Columbia International University
Columbia, SC 29203

PROPHETIC WITNESS PUBLISHING HOUSE
Upperton House, The Avenue, Eastbourne, Sussex,
BN21 3YB
1974

© F. A. Tatford.
First published in 1974.

Printed by Errey's Printers, High Street, Heathfield, Sussex.

TWENTIETH CENTURY SERIES

Twentieth Century Prophet. A biography of Dr. Fredk. A. Tatford, with a selection from his writings.

Prophet from the Euphrates. Balaam and his parables.

Prophet of a Broken Home. Hosea and his prophecy.

Prophet of Judgment Day. An exposition of Joel.

Prophet of Social Injustice. An exposition of the book of Amos.

Prophet of Edom's Doom. An exposition of the prophecy of Obadiah.

Prophet of Assyria's Fall. An exposition of the book of Nahum.

Prophet Who Deserted. The message of Jonah.

Prophet of Messiah's Advent. An exposition of the Book of Micah.

Prophet of the Watchtower. An exposition of the prophecy of Habakkuk.

Prophet of Royal Blood. An exposition of Zephaniah.

Prophet of the Restoration. Haggai and his message.

Prophet of the Myrtle Grove. The visions and prophecies of Zechariah.

Prophet of the Reformation. An exposition of the book of Malachi.

CONTENTS

	Page
PREFACE	9
1. INTRODUCTION	15
2. IRREVOCABLE PUNISHMENT	25
3. THE NARROWING CIRCLE	41
4. DIVINE GOODNESS IGNORED	53
5. THE FIRST DISCOURSE	59
6. THE SECOND DISCOURSE	71
7. THE THIRD DISCOURSE	81
8. THE THIRD DISCOURSE (continued)	97
9. PRIEST AND PROPHET	109
10. THE CORRUPT NATION	119
11. THE ULTIMATE BLESSING	129
BIBLIOGRAPHY	141

PREFACE

IN THE relative classlessness of the twentieth century, there is a tendency to forget the rigid distinctions of the Victorian era, when masters and servants belonged to very different classes economically, socially and educationally and even, to some extent, religiously (the rich worshipping at the church and the poor at the mission hall). The average employee deemed it utterly improper to disobey his employer or to render to him less than his total effort. Unreasonable demands and oppressive acts were accepted without murmuring because of the constant fear of losing employment.

Justice was not always plainly in evidence. In fact, it was frequently said—not entirely without justification—that there was one law for the rich and another for the poor. Certainly it seemed easier at times for the rich to evade their responsibility than for the poor to escape their liability.

The comparative luxury in which the upper class lived was in very great contrast to the stark poverty of many of the lower class, although the condescending charity of some well-meaning society ladies was not always accepted with the obsequious gratitude which might have been expected.

Generalisations are, of course, never completely accurate and the picture painted above may not be entirely true to life. But its essential features will probably not be questioned.

It was in days of class distinction, social injustice, oppression and immorality that Amos prophesied, and much of what he declared to Israel would have been appropriate to

Britain in the latter part of the nineteenth century. Yet his message is not entirely irrelevant to the present day. The problems may be different, but the basic attitude is the same, and the danger is as great. Justice, righteousness and the maintenance of proper standards are as essential today as they were two and a half millennia ago—and are just as clearly lacking. The herdman of Tekoa threatened judgment upon a guilty nation. Would he be less silent were he to be projected upon a twentieth century stage? Are today's conditions any less deserving of punishment?

Amos foretold famine, pestilence and sword. The judgments we are invoking may be of a different character, but they are equally inescapable. And we have gone too far to avoid the consequences of our folly. I take the liberty of quoting an article which appeared under my name in the January, 1974, issue of *Prophetic Witness*, which may not be inappropriate.

We are nearly three-quarters of the way through the twentieth century and it is not unreasonable to pause and take stock of the situation. Where have we reached and what has been achieved?

In 1973 there was an uneasy suspicion that we might well have been teetering on the brink of a third world war. Even when talks had opened regarding a cease-fire in the Middle East, there seemed no guarantee that Russia would not precipitate a holocaust which no one wanted and which everyone feared.

The threat of future trouble is no empty one. In the arsenals of the great powers there is a total explosive power equivalent to a million megatons of T.N.T. The stockpile of nuclear weapons is sufficient to destroy the whole of the population of the world 50,000 times over, and this takes no account of the suffering which might be inflicted earlier by bacteriological and biological warfare.

The problems of the present day are not merely military ones, however. The world is rapidly running out of the oxygen essential to life. Apart from human beings, every factory, car, ship and aeroplane reduces the supply. A 707 jet, for example, burns 35 tons of oxygen every time it crosses the Atlantic, while a jumbo jet consumes more than 50 tons of oxygen. And, at any one moment, around the world, there are over 3,000 jets in the air. Yet at the same time, we are thoughtlessly cutting down the forests which provide much of our oxygen. Dr. Lloyd Berkner pertinently utters the warning that we cannot hope to survive if we continue to behave as we are doing.

At present, 50 per cent of the population of the world have a food intake with a total calories content of less than 2,000 a day, 80 per cent. of Indian children suffer from protein deficiency. Yet the population goes on steadily increasing. In *The Environment Game,* Nigel Calder (formerly the editor of *The New Scientist*) questions whether man can last much longer unless he can replenish his food supplies. It is too late now to look to natural resources and, if world famine is to be avoided, it will be necessary to depend upon the chemical manufacture of food and particularly of proteins.

In *The Population Bomb,* Prof. Paul Ehrlich estimates that the population of the world will double itself in the next quarter of a century, and that the next half a century after that will create problems, not only of food, but of living space. Nature strongly resents overcrowding.

One of the greatest current problems is, of course, that of pollution. Dr. John Holloway, of Cambridge University, writing on this subject, asks, "How crazy can the world get? No rational man would actually set up conditions in which his very food and water were constantly polluted, his children killed and injured, and his whole environment rendered fouler all the time—not through his failures, but through his very efforts and so-called advances." One writer pertinently comments, "Man has fouled his own nest and will drown in his own sewage before the century is out." G. R. Taylor's *Doomsday Book* gives ample reasons for the doubts and uncertainties existing.

In his book, *Can Man be Modified?* Prof. Jean Rostand points out that we are culturing new viruses and seeking new mutants, but if a dangerous new mutant escaped, it could conceivably set off a universal epidemic, against which the population would be helpless since the natural defence systems would be unable to cope with it. This is not an empty dread. Prof. Salvador Lucia, a specialist in virology, frankly confesses to a feeling of tremendous fear regarding the future.

Prof. Bentley Glass declares that we may discover how to cultivate the reproductive cells of men and animals, to produce normal human embryos and raise them in artificial cultures. We may modify genetic features and improve genetic stock. We will soon be able to modify the mind and to enhance intelligence, to clone animals and men. But we may be making a bigger mistake than Prometheus when he stole fire from heaven to give to men. Sir Macfarlane Burnet, the Australian scientist who won a Nobel prize for his work on tissue transplants, aptly remarks, "It is becoming all too evident that there are dangers in knowing what should not be known." We may be prying into secrets hidden by the Creator.

By 2000 A.D. we will probably be generating electricity by solar cells. Hypersonic aircraft will be transporting us to Australia in an hour. Underground railways will blow pneumatic trains through tunnels with compressed air. We will carry small radio sets on our wrists like wristwatches, to receive and transmit messages. We will be using plastics in housing instead of wood and metal. We will be able to wear an exoskeleton to amplify our physical powers. We will have sperm banks for A.I.D., frozen embryos for prospective parents, and artificial placenta to avoid the disadvantages of the gestation period.

In his *Biological Time Bomb,* however, G. Rattray Taylor warns that the social disorientation resulting from biological developments may seriously undermine the social cohesion of western countries, and that the disorientation of society may lead to the disorientation of personality. "There are already signs of such personal nihilism in society today," he says, and it is particularly evidenced in the younger generation. The old mores are breaking up. In *Future Shock*, Alvin Toffler, approaching the matter from the angle of the rapid increase in knowledge, comes to very much the same conclusion. We are rapidly invoking the Divine judgment of which Amos spoke.

All in all, we are living in one of the most critical periods of history. The degree of instability is greater than ever it has been before and, on every side, people are asking what —*if anything*—the future holds. It is at such a time as this that we turn back to the reliable revelation of Holy Writ. Has the Bible a message for the present day? It has! The judgment of the guilty is inescapable, but the Bible declares categorically that the final solution to human and universal problems is in Jesus Christ, that peace will be brought to the warring nations by His intervention, that law and order will be restored to a disordered world by His power, that the hopes and aspirations of the human breast will be satisfied by His unveiling, that wrongs will be righted and evil checked by His restraint. The Scriptures disclose that the God-Man, Jesus of Nazareth, is to be the enthroned Sovereign of the universe, with every tongue acclaiming His worth. In that day, all will hail Him as King.

But these sacred pages also assert that the suffering church in China, the poverty-stricken Christian in India, the persecuted believer in Russia, the millions of waiting saints throughout the world, will soon behold the Saviour whom they adore. "For the Lord Himself will descend from heaven with a shout, with the voice of the archangel and the trump of God. And the dead in Christ will rise first. Then we who are alive and remain will be caught up together with them in clouds, to meet the Lord in the air. And so will we ever be with the Lord."

This is our hope and our confident expectation. Christ is coming—and coming soon! Today we bow in worship and adoration at His feet. Tomorrow we may stand in His presence and gaze upon His face.

> *I am waiting for the coming*
>   *Of the Lord who died for me,*
> *Oh, His words have thrilled my spirit,*
>   *"I will come again for thee."*
> *Faith can almost hear His footfall*
>   *On the threshold of the door,*
> *And my heart, my heart is longing*
>   *To be with Him evermore.*

FREDK. A. TATFORD.

CHAPTER 1

Introduction

A JUDEAN, called from the fields to prophesy mainly against the northern kingdom of Israel, having had no official training and no previous relationship with the prophetic line, Amos appeared upon the stage at one of the most critical periods of Israel's history. It was a day of peace and prosperity and the people were quite unaware of the stormclouds that were gathering beyond their northern frontier. They lived in the enjoyment of the material, with very little real thought for the spiritual.

Suddenly, upon the ears of the wealthy trader and the depressed peasant, there broke the voice of a herdman of Tekoa, with the proclamation of the justice and righteousness of God and His impending judgment upon those who ignored His standards. There seems to have been no positive reaction to his message. It was so completely out of harmony with the current conditions. There were no political indications of any threatening danger and, in their careless security, few were apparently conscious of the moral decay existing. Since there was no awareness of the sin and corruption of the nation, there was no apprehension of future retribution.

Although Amos came from the wilderness of the south, there is little doubt that he made annual visits to the markets of the north to dispose of the wool he had grown. Either in those centres or en route to them, he presumably met the traders of different countries with their great variety of merchandise, and he had obviously observed the slave traffic at first hand. He knew the religious shrines and festivals of Israel and was well aware of the common practices of the ruling class, which virtually invalidated their religious observances. He could not have been ignorant of the distress of the penurious peasant and the unconcern of the complacent aristocracy. The evidences of venal judges, avaricious traders and dishonest merchants were on every side. The self-indulgent, luxury-loving women, their rapacious and remorseless husbands, ready mercilessly to foreclose on the mortgage of the unfortunate smallholder, the perverted religionists who enjoyed their debauchery in the most sacred sites, all these and more met the perceptive eye of the man whose training had been under the tutelage of God on the hills of Judah. The knowledge of the conditions of Israel, acquired during those annual visits, were part of the equipment of the man for the ministry to which he was later called.

Although his message was primarily to Israel, Amos had been taught the lesson that "God's rule extends to all nations and that the standard by which the nations are judged is the standard of absolute justice" (P. H. Kelley, *Amos: Prophet of Social Justice*, p. 18). Because the nations surrounding Israel had disregarded that standard, he pronounced judgment upon them. Because of Israel's guilt and her more favoured position, he revealed that God was no respecter of nations and that punishment would be meted out to sinful Israel as justly as to her neighbours.

THE MAN

Little is known of Amos other than what is contained in his book. No other person of his name is mentioned in the Old Testament. (The name of Isaiah's father, quoted in Isa. 1 : 1, is not, of course, identical.) One other of the same name is mentioned in Luke 3 : 25. His name means simply a burden-bearer or load-carrier, but whether it had any special significance in the prophet's history or personality is not apparent. He gives bare details of himself and his occupation and reference is made to these in the next chapter. He was pre-eminently a man of the wilderness. As J. Paterson remarks, "The wide open spaces in which he lived are reflected in the amplitude of his spiritual vision. . . . All his similes and metaphors reflect the bare gaunt background of the desert. His task too was his teacher. He must be quick to detect the rustle of the gliding snake and know the way of the lion and the bear. Every sound in the desert is significant, and the shepherd must know its meaning. . . . The desert was the school of Amos, and in that school his powers of observation were developed and his faculties sharpened in high degree."

We are told nothing of the prophet's subsequent history. Contrary to the usual view that, after the altercation with Amaziah, the high priest of Bethel (Am. 7 : 12-17), Amos departed from Israel and returned to the land of Judah, there is a tradition that he died shortly after his prophecy concerning Amaziah and in consequence of the high priest's brutality. It is claimed that Amaziah was so angered by the prophet's reaction and particularly by his prediction of the disasters to befall the priest and his family, that he physically assaulted Amos and so belaboured him with blows that the unfortunate victim was carried back to his own country half-dead and succumbed to his wounds a few days later and was buried with his father.

There is no real evidence for the story, however, and it is more probable that the remainder of the prophecy was recorded after the intervention of Amaziah and that the prophet's return to Judah did not take place immediately. But no further information is given in the inspired record.

BACKGROUND

The period covered by the Book of Amos was one of political stability and prosperity for Israel. Jeroboam II and his predecessors had routed their foes and had laid tribute on several of the neighbouring countries. Damascus and Hamath had been captured and possession had been regained of all the land previously taken by Syria. No further trouble was to be expected from that quarter. Moreover, Egypt had been weakened by internal dissension and she constituted no threat to Israel's peace. The country was quiet and undisturbed and the nation was at the zenith of its power.

All the principal trade routes from Syria and Mesopotamia to Egypt and the Red Sea passed through Israel, and tolls were levied by Samaria on every caravan of merchandise. The traders came from all parts of the eastern world and the city consequently became a vast emporium of goods of every conceivable kind. The rapidly developing commercial activities and the growing financial profit resulting therefrom inevitably led to the nation's transition from the long-existing agricultural and pastoral mode of life to a commercial and industrial one.

Increasing urbanisation and the concentration of wealth in the cities reacted detrimentally upon the countryside and depressed the status and fortunes of the farm labourer and peasant. Contrary to the intention of the Mosaic law, family inheritances were often mortgaged to the wealthier and, in due course, acquired completely by them, so that a new class of rich landowners sprang up. The poorer, having forfeited the title to their lands, found themselves obliged to work for their creditors on fields which were previously their own property.

The whole social structure was disrupted. The middle class almost completely disappeared, leaving only the rich (who grew steadily richer) and the poor (who just as steadily grew poorer). In addition to the economic inequalities, which accentuated class distinctions in a country which previously had known none, there was a complete indifference to the plight of the poor. It was quite common for the debtor to be sold into slavery and possibly transported to another country from which there was no hope of return.

The rich merchant princes added to their wealth by unscrupulous commercial practices and merciless oppression of those less privileged than themselves. Not only was there social injustice; bribery and corruption in the law courts ensured that legal verdicts favoured the affluent and influential; the innocent man, who was unable to offer a gift to the judge, was doomed to lose his case.

In contrast to the humble dwellings of the poor, the new aristocracy built themselves winter and summer residences of hewn stone, with every form of comfort and luxury. Their tables were furnished with the best meats and wine, and they reclined on silk cushions on their ivory couches, their meals accompanied by the strains of every variety of music.

Despite the moral decadence which existed, there was a punctilious observance of religious requirements. Tithes and offerings were offered far in excess of those specified in the law; pilgrimages were regularly made to the religious centres of Israel and even to Judah; and, confident in their covenant relationship with Jehovah, the people faced the future without fear. But their religion had no effect upon their attitude to their fellow-men; it had no reflection in their conduct. As J. Paterson says (*The Goodly Fellowship of the Prophets,* p. 25), "The ethic of the thing done had been substituted for the ethic of the clean heart; religion had become externalised and materialised." Idolatry had been suppressed, but the sacred prostitution of the false religions was practised at the very shrines where Jehovah was allegedly worshipped.

DATE

The opening verse of the book indicates that Amos's ministry occurred during the reigns of Uzziah, king of Judah, and Jeroboam II, king of Israel. There has been considerable controversy regarding the dates of the rulers of Israel and Judah, but it is probable that Uzziah's long 52 years' reign commenced in 792 or 791 B.C. and that he died in 740 B.C. When he contracted leprosy, however, his son

Jotham became regent—possibly from about 748 B.C. The reign of Jeroboam II seems to have been from 793 B.C. to 753 B.C., although F. F. Bruce considers the period 782 B.C. to 745 B.C. to be more accurate. Whatever dates are taken, it is clear that the two monarchs reigned contemporaneously for a long period, and it is impracticable to deduce the date of the prophecy from this.

The same verse, however, declares that Amos's public mission commenced two years before an earthquake. No date is given for this event, but that it was a remarkable occurrence is clear from the further reference to it in Zech. 14 : 5. It is known that a total eclipse of the sun occurred on June 15th, 763 B.C., and C. T. Francisco, in *Introducing the Old Testament*, argues that Amos 4 : 13 associated the earthquake with the eclipse (see also Am. 8 : 8; 9 : 5), Josephus (*Ant.* ix, 10, 4) states that the earthquake occurred when Uzziah entered the temple to burn incense upon the golden altar (2 Chron. 26 : 16-21). The impious king was at that time smitten with leprosy and remained a leper until the end of his life. Unfortunately, the eclipse was in 763 B.C., whereas the date on which Uzziah was superseded by his son was probably about 748 B.C. It is, therefore, impossible to deduce precisely when the prophecy commenced.

The conditions described in the Book of Amos, deplorable although they were ethically and socially, show that the country was at peace and enjoying the prosperity resulting from the political and commercial expansion of Israel. The menace of the Assyrians under Tiglath-Pileser III had not yet made itself evident, and the period was presumably the middle of Jeroboam's reign.

Both Hosea and Jeremiah refer freely to Amos's book and it is generally thought that the former was a younger contemporary of Amos and commenced his ministry a little later. It is possible that Amos was also a contemporary of Joel. He certainly revealed an intmate knowledge of Joel's prophecy. Amos 1 : 2 is obviously a quotation of

Joel 3 : 16, and there is a clear reference to Joel 3 : 18 in Amos 9 : 13. The whole of the prophecy of Amos virtually falls between those two verses of Joel 3. Amos confirmed Joel's prophecy and, in greater detail, showed its implication. Since, however, there is little indication of the date of Joel's prophecy, this does not help in determining the date of Amos's book.

PURPOSE OF BOOK

Amos had only one task—to prophesy against Israel (Am. 7 : 15)—and his book is occupied primarily with that nation. Since he was a Judean, it is surprising that he should have been chosen for the purpose, but his ministry was exclusively to Israel and he does not seem to have prophesied at all in his own country of Judah. He portrayed the judgment of God sweeping in a series of concentric circles through the nations around until finally the circle shrank to the confines of Israel and judgment was poured out in its fulness upon that guilty people.

Humanly speaking, Amos's inspiration arose from the words of his contemporary, Joel. As Schlier (*Minor Prophets*, p. 70) says, "With a single word Joel arouses Amos; it is, as it were, the test of his whole prophecy, the substance of all his utterances; and what he declared was the thundering voice of God's judgment upon His people. A frightful storm comes down on Israel; we see the lightnings flash hither and thither from one people to another, till at last the gloomy storm-clouds stand over Israel and discharge themselves upon their guilty heads."

STYLE

Amos was the first of the prophets to commit his messages to writing, and his book is marked by its perfect symmetry, its apt choice of expression, the vividness and originality of its imagery, and the obviously close acquaintance of the author with the letter and spirit of the law. Jerome declared that the prophet was rude of speech. His rustic background and the dialect of those among whom he lived may have been reflected in some of his words, but his thoughts soared into the heights to give a fresh concept of God and His authority and administration among the nations. As C. Kuhl (*The Prophets of Israel*, p. 59) says, "From his acquaintance with geography, history, . . . legendary and proverbial wisdom . . . it is obvious that he was not an uneducated yokel."

He employed prose and poetry to serve his purpose, and drew upon every figure of speech to make his message clear. J. L. Mays (*Amos*, p. 6) writes, "His speeches display a remarkable skill at using all the devices of oral literature available in Israel's culture. . . . He was specially adept at the employment of forms of spech that appear in the riddles, comparisons and popular proverbs of folk wisdom. . . . Many of his metaphors come from observation of the country life which he knew as shepherd and farmer (1 : 3; 2 : 13; 3 : 12; 4 : 1; 9 : 9). But countryman from Tekoa though he was, his rich and polished speech warns that he is not be taken for a simple and unlettered person. No prophet surpasses him in the combination of purity, clarity and versatility that characterises his language." W. Robertson Smith describes the book of Amos as "one of the best examples of pure Hebrew style. The language, the images, the grouping, are alike admirable," he declares, "and the simplicity of diction . . . is a token, not of rusticity, but of perfect mastery over a language."

Whether his messages were recorded at the time of their utterance or were collated on his return to his own country is not clear. His book certainly bears the marks of careful composition and arrangement of material, but this does not necessarily imply the recording of his speeches subsequent to their actual delivery.

ANALYSIS

The book falls readily into three broad divisions, with a brief prologue and epilogue. The announcement of the forthcoming judgment to fall upon eight nations is followed by three discourses on the transgressions of Israel and then by five visions disclosing the inevitability of the punishment of the chosen race.

It may be analysed as follows:—

1. Prologue (1 : 1, 2).
2. The Judgment of the Nations (1 : 3—2 : 16).
   (a) Syria (1 : 3-5).
   (b) Philistia (1 : 6-8).
   (c) Phoenicia (1 : 9, 10).
   (d) Edom (1 : 11, 12).
   (e) Ammon (1 : 13-15).
   (f) Moab (2 : 1-3).
   (g) Judah (2 : 4, 5).
   (h) Israel (2 : 6-16).
3. The Transgressions and Punishment of Israel (3 : 1—6 : 14).
   (a) First discourse (3 : 1-15).
   (b) Second discourse (4 : 1-13).
   (c) Third discourse (5 : 1—6 : 14).
4. The Prophet's Visions (7 : 1—9 : 10).
   (a) Destruction by locusts (7 : 1-3).
   (b) Judgment by fire (7 : 4-6).
   (c) The plumb-line (7 : 7-9).
   (d) Amaziah's opposition (7 : 10-17).
   (e) The basket of summer fruit (8 : 1-14).
   (f) The altar of Bethel (9 : 1-10).
5. Epilogue (9 : 11-15).

The book was patently planned by Amos as one coherent whole, even if penned in sections. Keil (*The Twelve Minor Prophets*, vol. 1, p. 238) suggests that, "just as the close of his book points back to the introduction (chapters 1 and 2), so also do the visions of the second part correspond to the addresses of the first embodying the substance of the addresses in significant symbols. The parallel between the fifth vision and the elegy struck up in ch. 5 : 1 is very conspicuous; and it is also impossible to overlook the material agreement between the first and second visions and the enumeration in ch. 4 : 6-11 of the divine visitations that had already fallen upon Israel; whilst the third and fourth visions set clearly before the eye the irrevocable character of the judgments with which the careless and wanton sinners are threatened in chapters 3 to 6."

CHAPTER 2

Irrevocable Punishment

THE fundamental cause of the social, economic and political malaise of Israel was probably religious. The schismatic worship of Dan and Bethel (and possibly Beersheba in Judah) coupled with that of Baal introduced by Ahab (1 Kings 16 : 31), had seduced the people from the pure service of Jehovah at Jerusalem. Yet there was at least a nominal recogition of the claims of God.

When, on the death of Solomon, the ten northern tribes seceded to form the kingdom of Israel, the political schism was followed by a religious one. To obviate the people going up to Jerusalem to offer sacrifices and to observe the festivals, Jeroboam I made two golden calves and set up one at Dan for the inhabitants of the northern part of his realm, and the other at Bethel for those in the south. He appointed his own priesthood and apparently aranged a calendar of festivals on similar lines to that in force in Jerusalem (1 Kings 12 : 27-33). Amaziah appropriately, therefore, referred to Bethel as a royal sanctuary (Am. 7 : 13).

The sanctuary at Dan had been established long before, first as a domestic chapel for the worship of Jehovah by an Ephraimite named Micah (Jud. 17) and later in the city by the Danites (Jud. 18 : 30, 31), where it continued until the Assyrian conquest.

That at Bethel had an even longer history. An altar was erected there by Abraham four millennia ago (Gen. 12 : 8), and Jacob subsequently followed his example (Gen. 35 : 1-7).

Later it was recorded that the ark of the covenant was located there and that sacrifices to Jehovah were offered there and that pilgrimages were made to the sanctuary (Jud. 20 : 18, 26-28; 21 : 2; 1 Sam. 10 : 3).

Dan and Bethel were, therefore, obvious sites when Jeroboam I decided to set up schismatic altars.

The Canaanitish deity, Baal, was symbolised by a bull and although Jeroboam's two golden calves were evidently not intended as a representation of either Baal or Jehovah (any more than were the cherubim in the temple at Jerusalem), there was obviously a grave risk of the worshippers confusing the object and the ultimate possibility of syncretism and idolatry. Moreover, it was not long after that Abijah accused the king of setting up other gods (1 Kings 14 : 9).

Nevertheless, it was not the basic apostasy which God condemned as much as the insincerity and inconsistency of Israel's religious observances. The Divine denunciation, however, was sweeping and covered every aspect of the people's life, and the messenger chosen was eminently suitable for the task of denouncing the evils and announcing the impending judgment. Amos was no ordinary prophet. H. Hailey (*Commentary on the Minor Prophets*, p. 83) declares, "There was not in Amos the sympathy, warm love, and feeling of the statesman or citizen, but a cold sense of justice and right. Not a sob is to be found in his book for the nation of wicked apostates, and there is only a sigh for the poor. . . . He was the stern prophet of justice, and righteousness. His very attitude breathes the air of his life's rugged desert environment." Yet he was the unexpected messenger of Jehovah.

KEEPER OF FLOCKS

The words of Amos, who was among the shepherds of Tekoa, which he saw concerning Israel in the days of Uzziah king of Judah, and in the days of Jeroboam, the son of Joash, king of Israel, two years before the earthquake (1 : 1).

Referring to his origin, Amos said that he was "among the shepherds of Tekoa." The word *noked* used for "shepherd" was not the one commonly employed. It was applied to Mesha, king of Moab, in 2 Kings 3 : 4 in the sense of a sheep-owner or sheep-master and it has been inferred therefrom that the prophet may have been the owner of flocks of sheep and a man of some status in the community, but this does not necessarily follow. Indeed, in Am. 7 : 14, 15 he described himself as a "herdman"—inferentially an employee of the owner of the herd or flock—and that Jehovah called him "from following the flock."

The word *noked* was used of those who tended a special variety of sheep, commonly described as *nakad* and, in fact, still known by that name in Arabia. They were dwarfs in size and ugly in appearance, but their wool was highly prized as of the greatest value.

In Am. 7 : 14 he described himself also as a pincher of sycomores. A form of fig-tree, the sycomore flourished in the plains and did not grow on the hillside, so that Amos must have periodically left his accustomed occupation on the hills to engage in his secondary activity. The sycamore was appreciated both for its wood and its fruit.

Tekoa, the home of the prophet, was six miles south of Bethlehem and nearly 12 miles from Jerusalem, located on a hill over 2,500 feet above sea level. The city was incorporated in a system of border fortifications by Rehoboam (2 Chron. 11 : 6), although it clearly existed before that date. The rolling plain which stretched out at the foot of the hill was known as the wilderness of Tekoa (2 Chron. 20 : 20). The view from Tekoa was of a dreary and savage world: except for a glimpse of the blue waters of the Dead Sea, there was little more for the eye to rest upon but limestone hills and rugged mountains. "Upon this unmitigated wilderness, where life is reduced to poverty and danger," writes George Adam Smith (*The Book of the Twelve Prophets*, vol. 1, p. 76), "where nature starves the imagination, but excites the faculties of perception and curiosity; with the mountain tops and the sunrise in his face, but above all, with Jerusalem so near, Amos did the work which made him a man."

It was from Tekoa that Joab brought the "wise woman" to intercede with David for his son, Absalom (2 Sam. 14 : 2). "She understood," writes H. W. Wolff (*Amos the Prophet*, pp. 77, 78), "how to introduce a legal case (v. 6f); how, by use of an analogy from nature, to elevate it to the level of a principle, especially with regard to the rights of an outcast (v. 14); and how at the end to come to the choice between good and evil (v. 17)." The proverbial wisdom of Tekoa may well have been assumed because of this particular incident.

The prophet used a peculiar expression when he stated that these were the "words . . . which he saw concerning Israel." The Septuagint renders the clause, "words . . . which came to him in vision." Whatever interpretation is placed upon the expression, it is clear that he was claiming that the message was given to him, either by direct inspiration or by vision.

Amos dated his prophecy two years before the earthquake. Comment has been made upon this event in the preceding chapter. Josephus, who associated it with Uzziah's attempt to offer incense in the temple of Jerusalem, said that "a great earthquake shook the ground and, the temple parting, a bright ray of the sun shone forth and fell upon the king's face, so that forthwith the leprosy came over him. And before the city, at the place called Eroge, the western half of the hill was broken off and rolled half a mile to the mountain eastward, and there stayed, blocking up the ways on the king's gardens." It is interesting that excavators at Hazor discovered traces of an earthquake, which they dated in the eighth century B.C.

THE VOICE OF GOD

He said, Jehovah roars from Zion and utters his voice from Jerusalem; and the pastures of the shepherds mourn and the summit of Carmel withers (1 : 2).

The first half of verse 2 is a direct quotation of Joel 3 : 16 and shows how clearly both prophets realised that Jehovah's earthly dwelling-place was in the temple on Zion and that

His power was manifested in Jerusalem. The words were an implicit condemnation of the schismatic sanctuaries of Israel: these were not where God had placed His name.

Daringly Amos pictured the Almighty as a lion leaping upon his prey. The lion makes no noise while it is stalking its prey; its frightening roar reverberates through the countryside when the prey is within its power and is now about to be seized. In like manner, the prophet implied, Jehovah had burst into human affairs in judgment. Although they paid superficial homage to Him and brought to Him their offerings and sacrifices, their tithes and freewill gifts—and to a greater extent even than required by the law—He knew their hearts and the inconsistency of their lives. Previous warnings had been ignored, but now the day of reckoning had come. His roar would be heard from Zion.

His voice would sound forth from Jerusalem in rolling thunder. Driver (*The Books of Joel and Amos*, p. 127) says, "it was the Hebrew idea that, in a thunderstorm, Jehovah descended and rode through the heavens enveloped in a dark mass of cloud: the lightning flashes were partings of the cloud, disclosing the brilliancy concealed within, . . . and the thunder was His voice."

The Divine wrath swept over the pasture-lands of Israel in scorching drought, shrivelling up the food of the animals and consequently the hopes of men. It reached up to the great bold headland of Carmel 1200 feet above the sea into which it thrust and withered the thick woods and massed vegetation on the top of the promontory. The prophet spoke as though the threat was already in process of implementation, but it was presumably not yet a *fait accompli*. The storm-clouds were on the horizon and were now beginning to circle round the adjoining nations.

THE CRUELTY OF SYRIA

Thus says Jehovah, For three transgressions of Damascus, and for four, I will not revoke its punishment; because they have threshed Gilead with iron threshing instruments. So I will send fire into the house of Hazael, which will destroy the strongholds of Benhadad. I will break the bar of Damascus, and will cut off the inhabitants from the valley of Aven and him who holds the sceptre from Beth-eden. And the people of Aram shall go into exile to Kir, says Jehovah (1 : 3-5).

In each announcement of punishment, the phrase "for three transgressions and for four," was used. This indictment did not, of course, imply that the only crimes being brought under review were restricted to three or four. It is rather a formula, indicating that there had been a multiplicity of offences and that the measure of guilt was full. The crimes were not detailed in any of the eight oracles: one only was selected in each case, but each of these was a crime against humanity.

In each case also the phrase occurred, "I will not revoke it." The reference is undoubtedly to the punishment which had already been determined upon the guilty nation. The decision taken in the courts of heaven was now irreversible. The flagrant transgressions could no longer be tolerated: judgment could no longer be averted. "Seldom," said Horace, "has punishment with lingering foot parted with the miscreant, advancing before." That was certainly true now.

The first nation to hear its fate was Syria, one of Israel's ancient foes. The message was addressed to the Syrian capital, Damascus, reputed to be the oldest city in the world and to have been founded by Uz, the grandson of Shem. It was a wealthy, commercial city, through which the merchants' caravans constantly passed from the interior of Asia to the Mediterranean Sea. It stood in a broad plain, surrounded by orchards and cornfields watered by the River Barada, and was famed as a town of great beauty.

Sentence was pronounced upon Damascus for one particular atrocity. Because of Israel's sin, God had permitted the Syrians under Hazael and his son Benhadad to ravage the area east of the Jordan, including the land of Gilead. The forces of Israel were almost completely destroyed for, according to the inspired record, "the king of Syria had destroyed them, and had made them like the dust by threshing" (2 Kings 10 : 32, 33; 13 : 7).

This was evidently intended to be taken literally, for the transgression of which Damascus was accused was that they had "threshed Gilead with iron threshing instruments." The Syrians had apparently bound their captives and had treated them as they would have dealt with corn. Heavy boards, into the undersides of which had been driven iron spikes and jagged pieces of basalt, were drawn by horses over the threshing-floor to separate the grain from the chaff. These sledges were driven over the prostrate Gileadites, mangling and tearing their flesh from the bones in atrocious barbarity. The sadistic brutality seems almost incredible, especially as it was the action, not of blind savages, but of a civilised people.

Other acts of inhumanity had occurred in the conflict of four or five decades before, but retribution now came upon the nation primarily for this one crime of outstanding cruelty. Jehovah was not merely the God of Israel: He was Sovereign of the universe, and the nations were accountable to Him for their conduct. Taylor (*The Minor Prophets*, p. 28) appropriately maintains that "Men do not have to know the full revelation of God's law to come under His condemnation: they only have to violate the standards that they, in their relatively unenlightened state, can yet recognise (cf. Rom. 1 : 18-20; 2 : 12)."

For the crime of which they were indicted, the Syrians were to suffer the judgment of God. He declared that He would send a fire into the house of Hazael, which would destroy the strongholds of Benhadad. The symbol of fire in the O.T. was usually indicative of the flame of war. This was certainly the subsequent experience of the Syrians at the hands of the Assyrians. Damascus was captured, the king of Syria slain and the population carried away captive (2 Kings 16 : 9). The words may refer to the further sufferings of that country at a later date, and possibly even to her ultimate future fate.

Hazael, whose dynasty was to experience the immediate blast of Divine wrath, secured the throne by the murder of the ruling monarch (2 Kings 8 : 7-15), and he and his son, Benhadad III, showed their character in the manner in which they ravaged Israel (2 Kings 13:3). Hadad, the god of storms, was one of the deities of Damascus, and the kings of Syria normally assumed the name of Benhadad, and this had occurred in the case of Hazael's son.

The fiery devastation, which was to consume the house or dynasty of Hazael, was also to destroy the strongholds or fortifications of Benhadad. (The word "palaces" in the A.V. is not a very happy translation: the term used appears 27 times in the O.T. and usually in reference to fortifications). The implication of the Divine sentence was that the Syrian defences would be completely swept away and the security of the throne destroyed.

The bar of Damascus would be broken, declared Amos. The bar was simply the piece of bronze or iron (in some cases of wood) used to secure the city's gate. If that was smashed, nothing could stop the ingress of the invading foe, Damascus's defences would be broken and the inhabitants of the city would be at the mercy of the besiegers. Flight to other shelters would be rendered impossible. The fertile valley of Aven (often identified with Baalbek) might have provided refuge, but that way of escape was cut off. Betheden's luxurious palace might have afforded a refuge for the Syrian king, but his flight thereto was also cut off. There was no hope. The population of Syria were to be carried into exile to Kir (the place of their origin—see ch. 9:7); this is, of course, what actually occurred (2 Kings 16 : 9). God's word was meticulously fulfilled within a generation.

Some commentators interpret verse 5 as implying the extirpation of the inhabitants of the Aven valley because of the licentious idolatrous rites of Venus practised there, and also claim that the beautiful Betheden, at the foot of Hermon, was to suffer similarly for the evil practices followed in that area. There is some justification for that view, but it seems more probable that the prophet's intention was to indicate the utter hopelessness of Damascus under the hand of God. There could be no escape.

PHILISTIA'S SLAVE TRAFFIC

Thus says Jehovah, For three transgressions of Gaza and for four, I will not revoke its punishment; because they carried into exile an entire population in order to hand them over to Edom. So I will send a fire upon the wall of Gaza, which will destroy its strongholds. And I will cut off the inhabitants from Ashdod, and him who holds the sceptre from Ashkelon; and I will turn my hand against Ekron; and the remnant of the Philistines shall perish, says Adonai Jehovah (1 : 6-8).

The next country to come under sentence was Philistia and Gaza was selected as the representative city. Three other of her most important cities—Ashdod, Ashkelon and Ekron—were subsequently associated in the judgment upon their country. No reference was made to Gath, which was regarded as one of five great cities of Philistia. Gath was destroyed by Sargon II of Assyria in 711 B.C., but Amos' prophecy was earlier than that. The city may, however, have been captured by Judah prior to the date of the prophecy (see 2 Chron. 26 : 6) and may have been incorporated temporarily into that country. On the other hand, Amos specifically refers to it as a city of the Philistines in Am. 6 : 2. Each of these five principal cities had its own king, but they still remained part of the integrated whole and acted in agreement with each other.

Gaza, the capital of the country, was the southernmost city of Philistia, about three miles from the sea and on the edge of a great desert. It was located on the main trade route from Egypt to Tyre, but other roads also ran through it, so that it became an extremely prosperous city and its markets were filled with every conceivable commodity. It was also the centre of the slave traffic of Philistia. Gaza was a centre of idolatrous worship and the temple of Dagon was among its prominent buildings. Its reputation continued into Grecian times and seven temples of Greek deities were later to be found there. It was, of course, the scene of Samson's imprisonment and of his greatest feat (Jud. 16 : 21-30).

Ashdod was 21 miles north of Gaza and about the same distance (three miles) from the Mediterranean. It lay on the great caravan route from Joppa (now Jaffa) to Gaza and was strongly fortified. It was the chief seat of the worship of the Philistine god, Dagon, and it was in his temple that the ark of the covenant was placed after the defeat of the Israelites at Ebenezer in 1050 B.C. (1 Sam. 5 : 1, 2).

Ashkelon, the third in importance of the cities of Philistia, was situated on the coast, halfway between Gaza and Ashdod. It was the centre of the worship of Derceto, the fish-goddess. Tiglath-Pileser III made it a vassal city of Assyria in 734 B.C., but it was later sacked by Sennacherib. It was the birthplace of Herod the Great, who spent a large sum in beautifying the city.

Ekron, 12 miles north of Ashdod, was renowned as a city of idolatry. It was the seat of the worship of Baal-zebub (2 Kings 1 : 2), who was the god of flies.

The cities were admirably situated for their frequent attacks upon Judah. Pusey (*The Minor Prophets*, vol. 1, p. 246) says, "From Gaza lay a straight road to Jerusalem; but Ashkelon too, Ashdod and Ekron lay near the heads of valleys, which ran up to the hill-country near Jerusalem. This system of rich valleys, in which, either by artificial irrigation or natural absorption, the streams which ran from the mountains of Judah westward fertilised the cornfields of Philistia, afforded equally a ready approach to Philistine marauders into the very heart of Judah."

Jehovah pronounced an irrevocable judgment upon Philistia for a particularly callous example of her slave traffic. It was customary for captives in war to be regarded as the property of their captors and public conscience was not offended even if the captives were sold as slaves. But the charge made against Philistia was that, without any pretence of defending themselves or any excuse of war, they deliberately raided certain areas specifically in order to obtain slaves for sale. Their crime was of even darker colour for they completely depopulated some districts and swept the whole of the inhabitants into slavery, thereby robbing the aged and infirm— who were presumably left—of any hope of surviving. Then, acting as a middleman, they bartered their unhappy victims to Edom, which, in turn, would, of course, sell them to the highest bidders in their own or any other country (probably to the southern tribes of Arabia). Since Edom was the bitter enemy of Israel and Judah, the lot of the unfortunate victims could scarcely have been worse. This was professional slave-trading at its worst.

No indication is given of the actual occasion of the offence. Keil (*ibid*, p. 245) refers it to "the invasion of Judah by the Philistines and tribes of Arabia Petræa in the time of Joram, which is mentioned in 2 Chron. 21 : 16 and to which Joel had already alluded in Joel 4 : 3 et seq., where the Phoenicians and Philistines are threatened with divine retribution for having plundered the land and sold the captive Judeans to the Javanites (Ionians). . . . The Philistines sold one portion of the many prisoners, taken at that time, to the Edomites, and the rest to the Phoenicians, who disposed of them again to the Greeks." This, however, was probably only one example of what had become a regular means of obtaining revenue.

For what they had done, Jehovah declared that He would send a fire upon the wall of Gaza, which would destroy her fortifications or strongholds. It is probable that the reference was to the Assyrians as the instruments of God. In 743 B.C., Tiglath-Pileser III attacked Gaza and laid her under tribute. Three decades later the Philistine cities refused to pay the tribute required by Assyria, and in 711 B.C. Ashdod was destroyed and its inhabitants carried away captive. Ten years later, in consequence of their revolt, Ashkelon and Ekron suffered under the hand of Sennacherib.

This was precisely what had been predicted. God had threatened to cut off the inhabitants of Ashdod and the king of Ashkelon and to turn His hand in punishment against

Ekron. The cities suffered as foretold. But that was not the end. Philistia, as a nation, had determined its policy, and the nation must pay the price for its folly. "The remnant of the Philistines"—whoever had escaped the destruction suffered by the population of the chief cities—were to perish. The judgment of God was to fall in unmitigated wrath upon a guilty race.

PHOENICIA'S FORGOTTEN COVENANT

Thus says Jehovah, For three transgressions of Tyre and for four, I will not revoke its punishment; because they delivered up an entire population to Edom and did not remember the covenant of brothers. So I will send a fire upon the wall of Tyre, which shall destroy its strongholds (1 : 9, 10).

Turning northwards the review now brought into reckoning the country of Phoenicia and its principal city of Tyre. The Phoenicians were a seafaring race, given to commercial activities, and were a peace-loving people. Their country ran along the Mediterranean coast and Tyre was a seaport with two harbours, 35 miles north of Carmel. The Tyrians supplied a great deal of material for the temple built by Solomon at Jerusalem.

The accusation made against them was that they had delivered up an entire population to Edom. It was not suggested that they had taken captives in military action or by an unprovoked raid upon their neighbours. They had patently acted as agents for others who had themselves rounded up the whole of the population in an area, and had handed over the entire body of captives to the Edomites. The inhuman course could have been followed only in order to secure profit and it well deserved the condemnation announced.

The guilt was accentuated by the fact that the crime had been committed in face of a treaty existing between them and the nation which had suffered the loss of its people. Most commentators assume that the captives had been taken from Israel and purchased by the Phoenicians for resale, and that the covenant referred to was one between Tyre and Israel. Hiram I of Tyre and David were, of course, in commercial alliance, and Solomon also had a trading treaty with Tyre. It has also been suggested that the marriage of Ahab, king of Israel, with Jezebel of Phoenicia (1 Kings 16:31) established a relationship between the two countries. Israel and Edom owned a common ancestor in Abraham and one view taken is that it was this relationship which had been ignored by the Phoenicians. The significance, however, may have been no more than that the common rights of humanity —all men being brothers—had been violated.

If the slaves in question were Israelites, it was all the more regrettable that they should be sold to Edom. The Edomites were the inveterate enemies of Israel and Judah and had demonstrated their hatred on more than one occasion in the past. There is little doubt that they would take a vindictive delight in the acquisition of members of the hated race as their slaves. Phoenicia's crime was, therefore, all the greater, since she had delivered the unfortunate victims into the hands of those most likely to maltreat them.

For their action, God declared that He would send a fire upon the strongly fortified walls of Tyre, which would destroy her fortifications. The military activities of Ashurnasirpal II and later of Shalmaneser III of Assyria brought pressure upon Phoenicia to pay tribute to that country, and finally in 664 B.C. the Assyrians captured the city. It is more probable, however, that the judgment referred to in Amos was the destruction by Alexander the Great in 332 B.C., when 6,000 were slain and 30,000 sold as slaves. This was definitely the city's worst experience and well repaid them for delivering others to their Edomite enemies.

EDOM'S HATRED IN ACTION

Thus says Jehovah, For three transgressions of Edom and for four, I will not revoke its punishment; because he pursued his brother with the sword, and cast off all pity, and his anger endlessly tore to pieces, and he retained his fury for ever. So I will send a fire upon Teman, which shall destroy the strongholds of Bozrah (1 : 11, 12).

The Edomites were descended from Esau, although, by this time, other tribes had been absorbed as well. They occupied a mountainous country along the Arabah, the great depression running from the Dead Sea to the Gulf of Aqaba. The capital of the country was Sela, or Petra, but the prophet referred only to Bozrah in the north and Teman in the south —possibly to show the extent of the judgment about to fall.

Under the Mosaic law, the Israelite was obliged to recognise the blood relationship of Edom and Israel. Edom's land was not to be taken (Deut. 2 : 4, 5) and his posterity could become members of Israel in the third generation (Deut. 23 : 7, 8). Edom, on the other hand, displayed nothing but an implacable hatred against Israel. When the Israelites were making their journey to Canaan, the Edomites refused them passage through their country (Num. 20 : 14-21). They invaded Judah on more than one occasion and carried away captives. When Nebuchadnezzar invaded Judah and destroyed Jerusalem, instead of coming to the aid of their kith and kin, they rejoiced at their plight (Psa. 137 : 7) and later seized part of their territory. They were the inveterate foes of Israel and Judah. Far from displaying the sympathy and compassion of blood relations, they reneged on any obligation to them.

It is this to which Amos refers. Whether some specific occasion was in view or merely the general attitude of Edom to Israel, is not clear, but the description given was extremely appropriate, "He pursued his brother with the sword," declared Jehovah, "and cast off all pity, and his anger endlessly tore to pieces, and he retained his fury for ever." No respect for fraternal relationship produced compassion in his heart: he suppressed all pity. He pursued the people of Israel mercilessly, his only object being to slay and destroy. Nothing could affect his bitter animosity.

His anger against Israel was constantly raging; the expression employed was that relating to wild beasts. It tore uncontrolledly his very breast (Psa. 7 : 2) until it was unleashed in revengeful spirit against its object. He nursed his fury for ever: nothing could assuage it. He cherished it until some fresh opportunity arose of displaying it in action and gratifying his revenge.

The picture painted was a terrible one—more appropriate to beasts than to men—but it was a true description of Edom's attitude. The same spirit is not entirely missing today, even among Christians. Feelings are stored up until the occasion arises for bitterness to be poured out relentlessly. It scarcely needs to be said that this is not the spirit of Christ.

As in the case of the other countries, Jehovah declared that He would send a fire upon Teman, the strongly fortified city in the south, and that it would destroy the strongholds or fortifications of the equally strongly fortified city of Bozrah in the north. These cities represented the extremity of Edom's territory and the implication is that the judgment would encompass the whole land. The threat was implemented for the Edomites later suffered oppression first by the Assyrians and then by the Babylonians.

For those who see in the verses a picture of the Arabs of today, with their bitter antagonism to Israel, the words may have a still future application.

CHAPTER 3

The Narrowing Circle

THE cloud of judgment continued to sweep round the nations bordering on Israel and the people of that land must have rejoiced at the repeated declaration that sentence was passed upon these nations. It seemed only appropriate that these should come under the punitive hand of God, but Israel was in covenant relationship with Him and doubtless persuaded herself that evil would never be pronounced upon her. Yet the circle was narrowing, the noose was tightening.

AMMON'S WAR ON WOMEN

Thus says Jehovah, For three transgressions of the Ammonites and for four, I will not revoke its punishment; because they ripped up the pregnant women of Gilead, in order to enlarge their borders. So I will kindle a fire on the walls of Rabbah and it shall destroy its strongholds with shouting in the day of battle, with a tempest in the day of the whirlwind. And their king shall go into exile, he and his princes together, says Jehovah (1 : 13, 15).

The Ammonites were descendants of the incestuous son of Lot's younger daughter and occupied an area adjacent to the Moabites between the Arnon and Jabbok. They were consistently hostile to the Israelites and were often in alliance with other countries against them. Their capital was Rabbah, or Rabbath Ammon (now Amman), a very strong city on the east of the Jordan. This was the principal centre of the worship of the god Molech.

In order to secure a greater area for themselves, they had, at some unspecified time, made an attack upon Gilead in the attempt to take possession of its rich grazing land. This had happened on several occasions (e.g. Jud. 10 : 8; 1 Sam. 11 : 1) and there is no indication when the crime described actually occurred.

The accusation made against them was that, either on a particular occasion or as an habitual offence, on their northern border raids on Gilead, they had deliberately ripped open the pregnant Gileadite women. They were not alone in practising such sadistic and horrifying cruelty: as 2 Kings 8 : 12 indicates, it had been the practice of other nations also. The barbarity was not perpetrated in self-defence but for the express purpose of exterminating the whole of the inhabitants of Gilead and preventing them from repopulating the country. This was really the calculated murder of mothers and unborn children, merely for the purpose of extending the territory of Ammon.

But such an offence against humanity could not be allowed to go unpunished, and Jehovah threatened that He would kindle a fire upon the wall of Rabbah, which would destroy its fortifications. The strong citadel would collapse under the assault. The war-cries of their enemies would ring out as they pressed home the siege in the day of battle, and like a tempestuous storm the conquering armies would sweep over the city. The defeat was to be utter and complete. The fulfilment may have come when the country was attacked by the Syrians and later by the Babylonians, but the threat has certainly been fully implemented (see Ezek. 25 : 5, 10; Zeph. 2 : 9). In *The Land and the Book*, Thomson says, "Nothing but ruins are found here. . . . Not an inhabited village remains, and not an Ammonite exists on the face of the earth." Cruelty inevitably meets with retribution.

The prophecy declared that the king and princes of the Ammonites should go into exile together, their power presumably broken and their future one of humiliating servitude. It is possible, however, that the clause has a religious significance rather than a political one. The deity of Ammon was the cruel and vicious god, Molech or Milcom, and the word translated "king" may have referred to the god. Similarly the reference to "princes" may have been intended to indicate the priests of the false god. Both the Septuagint and the Peshitta versions, as well as some other translators, interpret the clause as referring to Molech and his priests. The evil system of idolatry was to be banished from the land.

CREMATING THE DEAD

Thus says Jehovah, For three transgressions of Moab and for four, I will not revoke its punishment; because he burned into lime the bones of the king of Edom. So I will send a fire upon Moab, and it shall destroy the strongholds of Kerioth; and Moab shall die amid tumult, amid shouting and amid the blast of trumpet. And I will cut off the ruler from its midst, and will slay all its princes with him, says Jehovah (2 : 1-3).

The Moabites were descended from the incestuous son of Lot's older daughter, and occupied an area to the east of the Dead Sea between the Ammonites and the Edomites and bordering on the river Jordan. They were not a particularly warlike people, although involved in conflict from time to time with Edom and Israel.

The Moabites were arraigned because they burned into lime the bones of the king of Edom. It is possible that this occurred during or after the joint campaign of Israel, Judah and Edom against Moab recorded in 2 Kings 3. The Moabites were being worsted in the battle and made a determined attempt to slay the king of Edom and, capturing his eldest son, offered him for a burnt offering (2 Kings 3 : 26, 27). It may be that the king of Edom was subsequently slain and that the burning of his corpse took place at that time.

It was commonly regarded as sacrilegious to deny burial to anyone. The outrageous treatment adopted by the Moabites was reserved for criminals (Gen. 38 : 24; Lev. 20 : 14; 21 : 9). To deal with the body of an enemy in such a fashion was an unpardonable indignity to the dead. Driver (*ibid*, p. 143) describes it as "a mark of unrelenting hate and vindictiveness: the Moabites pursued their fallen adversary even into the rest of the grave; they not only violated the sanctity of his tomb, but even removed his bones and treated them with an unwonted and shocking indignity (cf. 2 Kings 23 : 16)."

For what they had done, Jehovah declared He would send the fire of trouble upon Moab, which would destroy the strongholds or fortifications of Kerioth. The latter (referred to also in Jer. 48:24, 41) is named on the Moabite stone and it is thought to have been a new capital beyond the river Arnon. The end of Moab was to come amid the tumult and uproar of war, with war-cries mingling with the blast of the attackers' trumpets.

Their prospect was hopeless, for it was God's intention to cut off the ruler (not necessarily a king) and to slay all his princes or chief officers. Administration was to be destroyed and all authority broken. Moab was to meet with its deserts and it would disappear from view as a power.

THE REJECTED LAW

Thus says Jehovah, For three transgressions of Judah and for four, I will not revoke its punishment; because they have rejected the law of Jehovah and have not kept his statutes, and their falsehoods, after which their fathers walked, have led them astray. So I will send a fire upon Judah and it shall destroy the strongholds of Jerusalem (2 : 4, 5).

The storm-cloud was drawing nearer and the rolling thunder was now clearly audible. No longer was the prophecy directed at the Gentile nations. The southern kingdom of Judah was now called to account. The charge in this instance was not, as in the other cases, one of an offence against humanity and humane standards, but of one virtually against Jehovah Himself.

Above all other nations, Judah should have known the will of God and the standards He had set up for man. They were the repositories of the law: the Divine oracles had been entrusted to them; and they had the exponents of the law constantly in their midst. The *torah*, the totality of the commandments and instructions given by Jehovah as the rule of life, and the *chuqqin*, the individual precepts of the *torah*—the moral, legal and ceremonial commandments—were taught them by the priests. As Driver pertinently remarks (*ibid*, p. 230), "The general sense of 'law' in the Old Testament is *authoritative direction* . . . but the kind of 'direction' denoted by it varies with the context. Its principal and probably primary application is to *oral direction* given by the priests in Jehovah's name, on matters of ceremonial observance, e.g. on distinctions between clean and unclean, on the different species of sacrifice, and the cases in which they were respectively to be offered, on the criteria of leprosy, etc." But far more than this was at stake.

God declared that they had rejected (rather than "despised") His law and had not kept His statutes. In other words, the requirements of Jehovah were regarded as no longer relevant. Both written and oral law were not merely disregarded but quite deliberately rejected. The people were no longer prepared to accept the Divine standards as applicable to their lives and conduct, and they regarded the commandments enunciated by their leaders and priests as pettifogging irrelevancies, possibly more suitable for an earlier age than their enlightened day.

It is questionable whether they realised the seriousness of their attitude. Laetsch (*The Minor Prophets,* p. 144) comments that "their whole history was the record of their disobedience and despising of God's law and their following the lies, the falsehoods, the deceptions of lying prophets, who seduced them from God's truth to false doctrines, the inventions of sinful men. This unbelief, this contempt of God's truth, was sufficient cause for a punishment like that meted out by the God of justice to the wicked heathen." What made it the more deplorable was that they were the people of God, upon whom He had set His love and whom He had so signally blessed. Yet they could turn away from Him and treat His will as of no account.

Is this not a characteristic of our twentieth century too? Through the centuries the mercy and compassion of God have been amply demonstrated. His Word has been taught and His claims made clear. Yet, in general, men have hardened their hearts and refused to listen to His voice. Dr. Karl Menninger, a well-known American psychiatrist, has aptly entitled his recent book, *Whatever Became of Sin?* If God's commandments are no longer valid, there can be no sense of guilt at their transgression. Menninger pertinently writes, "Believers continued their beliefs, not only in a Creator, but in His displeasure at their moral failures. They confessed their sins in their own company, but they did not refer to them in daily life intercourse. Sin was no longer a topic of conversation, debate, argument, accusation, and public remorse, as it long had been. It was no longer a euphemism for masturbation, adultery, drunkenness, smoking or gambling. It became a word of mild disapproval, less and less frequently applied, or a jocular word." Today it may be questioned whether many Christians have a true appreciation of the heinousness of sin. And all this is due primarily to the loss of respect for God's Word.

Judah were condemned still further for "their falsehoods, after which their fathers walked," which had "led them astray." They had copied the evil practices of their forefathers. This was not in lying or deception of one another and not merely in the falsehood of their inconsistent conduct, reprehensible although that was. The term used applied to the false gods whom they and their fathers had followed—idols whose claim to authority and to power to help their adherents was completely false (2 Kings 17 : 15-17). As one writer puts it, these false gods were "fabrications and nonentities, having no reality in themselves and, therefore, quite unable to perform what was expected of them." To turn away from Jehovah to these empty things of the imagination was nothing less than an insult to God.

There could be only one outcome for these impenitent sinners. Jehovah declared that He would send a fire upon Judah and that it would devour the fortifications of Jerusalem. The Divine statement was soon verified, for within two centuries the Chaldeans took the city and destroyed it by fire (2 Kings 25 : 9). Centuries later the Romans captured Jerusalem and, after looting it, put everything to the flames. The defences were destroyed and not one stone of the city or of its glorious temple was left standing upon another. The hand of justice fell upon the guilty.

The prophet's audience, as he announced the fate of the surrounding nations, was, of course, the people of Israel. They would naturally have concurred completely in all that had been said and would have rejoiced at the misfortune of their neighbours—a justifiable misfortune in their eyes. But the circling cloud had stopped and now rested above their heads and, to their utter amazement, they heard their own doom.

ISRAEL'S SOCIAL MISCONDUCT

Thus says Jehovah, For three transgressions of Israel and for four, I will not revoke its punishment; because they sell the righteous for silver and the needy for a pair of sandals. They trample the head of the poor into the dust of the earth, and turn aside the way of the afflicted. And a man and his father go into the same girl, to profane my holy name: and they lie down beside every altar on clothes taken in pledge, and in the house of their gods they drink the wine of those who have been fined (2 : 6-8).

The case against Israel was clearly stated. It consisted of the oppression of the poor, sexual immorality and idolatry, cupidity and perversion of justice. P. H. Kelley (*Prophet of Social Justice*, pp. 42, 43) sees in the prophecy against Israel an excellent example of a covenant lawsuit. His comments are so apt that we quote *in extenso*. He argues that the lawsuit "is a device designed to restore a breach of covenant. . . . (cf. Isa. 1 : 2 ff; 3 : 13 ff; 5 : 1-7; Jer. 2 : 1 ff; Hos. 2 : 2 ff; Amos 3 : 1, 2, 9-15; 4 : 1 ff; Mic. 6 : 1 ff). These covenant lawsuits included some or all of the following elements: (a) a call to the witness to give an ear; (b) an introductory statement by the Divine Judge or His prophet; (c) a recital of the gracious and marvellous acts of God; (d) a recital of calamities and judgments in the recent past, which should have recalled the people to God; (e) the specific indictment; (f) the sentence. . . . The role of the prophet in these lawsuits is highly significant. They literally believe that they are officers of the heavenly court sent to announce that God's covenant has been breached and that radical judgment is forthcoming. After announcing the divine sentence, which is usually very short, the prophets may expound on this, categorising the sins of the people. Or they may undertake to substantiate their own call and authority to be prophets. At other times they engage in lamentation and intercession for the people."

It is evident from later sections of the Book of Amos that there was no consciousness of wrongdoing on the part of Israel, and the people must have been astounded that they should be placed in the dock by the side of their Gentile neighbours, whose guilt was more apparent. But Jehovah made it clear that they were equally culpable, even if for other reasons. Their sins were of a different character, but they rendered the people totally unworthy of association with God. They were religious, but their religion had no effect upon their conduct.

It was in their social behaviour that they particularly fell short. The law provided that a Hebrew who had become poor could sell himself for a period of six years (Deut. 15 : 12), but it gave no power to a creditor to sell an insolvent debtor. Yet this was what was being done. The Israelites were selling the impoverished man into slavery—and that for a few pieces of silver. God described the victim as "the righteous," so that it was patently through no fault of his own that he had fallen into debt. (The term "righteous" is, of course, used here in a forensic and not ethical sense.)

The accusation went still further and claimed that the poor or needy were being sold for a pair of sandals. If the sale was, in fact, merely to acquire a pair of sandals, the worthless price showed a regrettable contempt for the unfortunate victim. The term may, however, have some connection with the common practice of selling land by handing over a shoe (Ruth 4 : 7). The shoe was virtually the title-deed of the property. The wealthy man, in that case, was expropriating the family inheritance, which was, of course, in direct conflict with the law, since the intention was presumably to add it permanently to his own possessions.

The picture painted is one of heartless oppression of the poor, and God could scarcely remain silent when confronted with the injustices of these merciless merchants.

The A.V. of verse 7 implies that, not content with having dispossessed the unfortunate debtor of his hereditary property, the harsh Shylocks begrudged him even the dust which, in mourning for his loss, the poor man sprinkled on his head (Job. 2 : 12; 2 Sam. 1 : 2). Nothing was too small for the covetous. Many expositors have adopted this translation, but the consequent interpretation does not seem entirely satisfactory and it seems more appropriate to render, as suggested above, "trample the head of the poor into the dust of the earth." Having extracted everything from the poor debtor, the avaricious oppressor sought only to crush him completely, to grind him down into the dust, to trample him underfoot. The simile is an apt one for the oppression which was being practised.

These heartless persecutors of their less fortunate brethren were also accused of turning aside the way of the afflicted. Not content with reducing them to a state of misery, the arrogant upper class of the day sought only to thwart the meek and frustrate them in all their ways. Keil (*ibid*, p. 253) suggests that it means "to bring them into a trap, or cast them headlong into destruction by impediments and stumbling-blocks laid in their path. The way is the way of life, their outward course." This is quite a legitimate interpretation, but it is possible that the reference is rather to the maladministration of justice. The innocent man, haled into court by his relentless persecutor, may have been condemned as guilty by the venal judge and, as another has said, the term was "a locution for the perversion of legal procedure."

The accusation was also levelled against these Israelites that they not only oppressed the poor but were guilty of sexual immorality of a despicable character. It had become a practice for a man and his father even to have intercourse with the same girl. It has been suggested that the reference is to the use of a female slave as a concubine by both father and son, virtually an act of incest and prohibited by the law (Deut. 22 : 30). It is more probable, however, that what was described was temple prostitution since it was subsequently stated that the habit profaned Jehovah's name.

Laetsch considers that the sin was not necessarily with temple harlots, the *kedeshim*, since the Hebrew word merely relates to a girl, and she may not even have been a public prostitute. But in that case, the relationship with the altars (and consequently the temples) mentioned in the following verse would not be evident.

In many of the heathen cults, there were fertility rites in honour of a goddess and these involved sexual intercourse with the women serving the temple. In some cases, it was essential for every female worshipper to prostitute herself for the benefit of the goddess at some period of her life. The Israelites had evidently taken over this practice from the idolatrous systems of religion surrounding them and had even possibly made it a custom at the very sites set apart for the worship of Jehovah, although this is not clear. The enormity of the sin in this case lay in the fact that father and son were resorting to the same woman and in the precincts of the temple or sacred site itself. For a prostitute to be offering herself indiscriminately at a site set apart to Jehovah was in itself an abomination to God and this was magnified by the incestuous conduct (which apparently had become habitual). It was an audacious violation of the holiness of Jehovah.

It seems incredible that any could have been so blind as

not to realise the implications or to appreciate the dishonour done to the name of God. The prophecy almost implies that the action was taken deliberately in order to profane His holy name. It was certainly the inevitable result.

More was to follow. The adulterers stretched themselves out by the side of the altar, as if nothing was sacred, and lay down with their willing partners on garments taken in pledge from their debtors. Garments were at times used as a pledge of a debt but, if a debtor entrusted his outer garment or cloak to his creditor, the latter was under legal obligation to return the *salmah* to its owner before sundown (Ex. 22 : 26, 27). The cloak, thrown around a man by day, was his covering at night: among poorer people, it was his only covering. It was a contravention of the law, therefore, for the creditor to retain it overnight. Yet these callous wretches not only ignored the need of the poor, but used their very clothes as a bed for their adultery.

Not content with such flagrant violation of the rights of their fellow-men as well as of the law, they conducted their carousals in the same sacred sites, using wine bought with fines paid by those condemned by the law court. There was no justice at the court: they bribed the judge to secure a verdict against those whom they prosecuted and, with the fines levied upon the condemned (who, in fact, were often innocent of the crimes for which they had been punished), they purchased the wine for their drunken debauches.

This, Jehovah declared, they did "in the house of their gods." It might be inferred from this that the whole of the contemptible procedure occurred in a temple of the false gods —as it may quite well have done. On the other hand, there may be an ironical disowning by Jehovah of the sites allegedly sanctified to Him and an indirect indication that they were no better than the temples of the heathen.

Were sins of the character described to be regarded as comparable to the inhumanity and evil conduct of the nations upon whom sentence had been pronounced? It seems that God was more concerned with the insincerity and inconsistency of those who named His name than with the grosser sins of the Gentiles who did not know Him. The profession of trust in Jehovah involved a life in accordance with His will, but the conduct of Israel was completely out of harmony with His stated will.

CHAPTER 4

Divine Goodness Ignored

HAVING arraigned Israel for the manner in which the people's life and conduct dishonoured Him, Jehovah turned to the benefits He had bestowed upon them, setting in stark contrast His blessing and their base ingratitude and reluctance to implement His will in their lives. The lesson is one which might well be conned by many of God's people of another day. His blessings are not to be selfishly appropriated, with a blind disregard for others. The grace of God should transform the lives of the people and, as a result, attract others to Him.

DISPOSSESSION OF THE AMORITE

Yet I destroyed the Amorite before them, whose height was like the height of the cedars, and he was as strong as the oaks: I destroyed his fruit above and his roots beneath, I also brought you up out of the land of Egypt, and led you forty years in the wilderness, to possess the land of the Amorite (2 : 9, 10).

The Amorites were descendants of the fourth son of Canaan and were among the early inhabitants of that country. Prior to its invasion by the Israelites, the Amorites occupied the territory on both sides of the river Jordan. They were so prominent in the land that their name was often used to represent the whole of the inhabitants of Canaan.

The name means "the high one" and M. F. Unger suggests that this was given to them because of their occupation of the highlands (Deut. 1 : 7, 19, 20), but they were not restricted to the mountainous area and the term "highlander" would be applicable to only a limited number. It is more probable that the term "high one" referred to their height. The giant sons of Anak (Num. 13:22, 32) apparently belonged to the Amorites, for example. Moreover, verse 9 specifically refers to the height of the Amorites.

God had promised the land of Canaan to Israel, but it was occupied by powerful nations, of whom the Amorites were one. Had Israel been dependent upon her own strength, her foes might well have proved invincible, but Jehovah declared that He destroyed them. The Amorites were figuratively as tall as the cedars and as strong as the oaks. They were well able to defend themselves, but they were destroyed root and branch—their fruit above and their roots beneath. This was indisputable and it was unthinkable that Israel should not acknowledge the power and the beneficence of the One who had so conspicuously acted on their behalf.

It was Jehovah who brought them out of the bondage of Egypt to give them possession of the land of the Amorites. When they demonstrated their unsuitability for immediate possession of the country, He led them for forty years through the wilderness, displaying His mercy and forbearance, until ultimately He brought them into the promised land. These were facts of which they were aware and were clear evidences of His grace and goodness. Was their conduct now a fitting recompense of His love or an evidence of their fidelity to Him?

SPIRITUAL NEEDS SATISFIED

I raised up of your sons for prophets, and some of your young men for Nazarites. Is it not even so, O you people of Israel? says Jehovah. But you gave the Nazarites wine to drink, and commanded the prophets, saying, Prophesy not (2 : 11, 12).

God provided not only for the material needs of Israel, but also for their spiritual needs. In order that they might know His will and be taught His requirements, He raised up prophets for them. These constantly portrayed the life of righteousness to the people, denouncing their sins and pleading with them to turn in repentance to God. The divine provision was intended to ensure that they walked in accordance with His will. Yet in their insensate folly, they had rejected the messages of the prophets and had endeavoured to silence them. Far from listening to the Word of God through their lips, they wanted nothing of prophets and bluntly told them to refrain from prophesying.

Young men had, under divine guidance, taken the vow of the Nazarite and had voluntarily assumed the threefold restriction. They lived before their fellows as those set apart to Jehovah, their abstentious and devoted lives a constant witness to Him. But, at the same time, their lives were, of course, an implicit protest against the self-indulgence, sensuality and worldliness of the rest of the people. This was patently resented and the Israelites reacted against the testimony of the Nazarites. One provision of the Nazarite vow was that no wine should be drunk during the whole of the period for which the vow was operative (sometimes, as in the case of Samson, this was for a whole lifetime). In unpardonable rebellion against the divine requirement, the people apparently pressed wine upon the Nazarites and induced them to drink.

Their hearts were hardened against God and they were determined to follow their own desires. It mattered not to them that they were in conflict with Jehovah: they had decided upon their course. His goodness and His examples had no effect. It was little wonder that the storm-clouds grew darker.

THE THRESHING CART

Behold, I am pressed under you, as a cart is pressed that is full of sheaves (2 : 13).

There is some doubt as to the correct translation of verse 13. The R.S.V., for example, renders it, "I will press you down in your place as a cart full of sheaves presses down." The Syrian version translates, on similar lines to the A.V., as "I am weary under your burdens, as a cart creaks that is full of sheaves."

The picture was of the threshing cart, which "consisted of three or more rollers set in a heavy wooden frame surmounted by the driver's seat. These rollers were attached to wheels on the outside of the framework, and if either the wheels or the rollers were clogged by the sheaves of grain over which the sledge was drawn by oxen, the sledge was stopped from further progress until the obstructing sheaves had been removed."

If the A.V. rendering is accepted, the implication is that Jehovah Himself was burdened by the sin of His people. It was for Him like the pressure of the fully loaded waggon on the harvest field, weighing down into the ground. Israel's transgressions and injustice so heavily burdened Him. He was weary with their evil ways.

If the alternative rendering is followed, it is a clear statement of the punitive action about to be taken. The full weight of Divine judgment would press down upon Israel relentlessly and unreservedly. They would feel the burden of God's hand upon them. This was their desert and it was now inescapable. The cup was full.

NO DELIVERANCE

Therefore, flight shall fail the swift, and the strong shall not retain his strength, nor shall the mighty save his life, He who handles the bow shall not stand; and he who is swift of foot shall not save himself; nor shall he who rides the horse save his life. And the stout-hearted among the mighty shall flee away naked in that day, says Jehovah (2 : 14-16).

The punishment which Israel was about to endure would be comprehensive: none would escape. When disaster threatened, the swift might normally flee to a secure refuge but, in this case, the runner's swiftness would be of no avail; his speed would evaporate and he would be unable to avoid the falling blow. The strong would naturally rely upon his strength in facing any who might assail, but now his strength would drain away and he would be completely unmanned in the presence of the mighty Judge. The well-equipped and trained warrior would expect to use his skill and ingenuity in warfare to defeat any opponent, but now he would face One against whom he was impotent: no effort of his own could deliver him.

The bowman would take his stance and fit his arrow to the string, but now he would be unable to keep his place; his weapon was of no value. Judgment would fall so quickly that the swift runner would be unable to escape before the blow fell, and the horseman would find himself equally unable to evade the trouble and save his life.

Jehovah was the rock and fortress of His people (Psa. 91 : 2). He was their refuge and salvation was in Him. They had rejected the Divine shelter, only to find that no other was available. Even the most courageous among the warriors, the stout-hearted among the mighty, could no longer defend themselves, and God depicted them as casting away their weapons, clothes and every encumbrance in the frantic endeavour to escape.

There was no escape. Within a few decades, the Assyrians, under Shalmaneser and then Sargon II, besieged and then captured Samaria and ransacked the city. The mills of God may grind slowly but nothing will stop them: the end is inevitable. It is a lesson we do well to learn. A refusal to listen to the Divine appeals and a resolute determination to pursue our self-chosen course can only have one end. The One with whom we have to do is supreme in every sphere.

It is interesting to note the manner in which all the predicted judgments upon the nations described in the Book of Amos were eventually fulfilled. The hand of the Almighty moved the nations of the world to implement His purposes. Pusey (*ibid*, p. 232) writes, "There followed, under Tiglath-Pileser, the fulfilment of the prophecy as to Damascus and Gilead. Under Sargon was fulfilled the prophecy on the ten tribes. That on Judah yet waited 133 years and then was fulfilled by Nebuchadnezzar. A few years later, and he executed God's judgments foretold by Amos on their enemies Moab, Ammon, Edom, Tyre. Kings of Egypt, Assyria, and the Macedonian Alexander fulfilled in succession the prophecy as to Philistia. So various were the human wills, so multitudinous the events, which were to bring about the simple words of the shepherd-prophet." What God had said He would do, He did, in fact, perform.

The first major section of the prophecy was complete. The remainder of the book concentrated upon Israel and her transgressions. The second major section presented three long discourses to God's people.

CHAPTER 5

The First Discourse

EACH of the three discourses which compose Amos 3, 4 and 5, commences with the formula "Hear this word" (3 : 1; 4 : 1; 5 : 1). A similar expression is used in Am. 7 : 14 and 8 : 4. Mays (*ibid*, p. 55) remarks, that this proclamation formula "creates a situation in which hearing is the commanded response; an otherwise occasional accident group is constituted and identified as those for whom the following message is meant." God demanded that attention should be given to His words.

THE PRIVILEGED NATION

Hear this word that Jehovah has spoken against you, O people of Israel, against the whole family which I brought up out of the land of Egypt, saying, You only have I known of all the families of the earth: therefore I will punish you for all your iniquities (3 : 1, 2).

Amos called upon the people to listen to the all-important principle which was about to be enunciated. In uninhibited self-satisfaction, Israel boasted of their election and covenant and confidently relied upon their favoured position as the pledge of their immunity from the punishment which fell upon other nations for their wrongdoing. They blindly ignored the ethical implications of the covenant and declined to consider their responsibility to live in a manner honouring to their Benefactor.

Jehovah reminded them that it was He who had brought

them (including Judah) up out of the land of Egypt and, of all the families or tribes of earth, they were the only one whom He had recognised as His own. It was His power which had delivered them from Egypt and rolled back the nations of the Red (or Reed) Sea on their behalf. In sovereign mercy He had chosen them out of all the nations of the earth to be His own.

This did not mean that they could live as they pleased and omit to fulfil the obligations incumbent upon them. This is the antinomian error of many Christians today, who consider that, secure in salvation wrought for them at Calvary, there is no obligation upon them to live as those who belong to Christ, and whose lives are strangely lacking in personal holiness and practical sanctification. Yet privilege always connotes responsibility as well.

God's election was no guarantee of Israel's exemption from punishment for wrongdoing. Their unique relationship to Him only established a more definite basis for accountability: there was a correlation of His election and their culpability. Because of their nearness to God, the nation *must* be punished for its iniquities. It was a Divine principle, which is still applicable today. The principle enunciated, was as another has suggested, virtually a paradigm of Amos's prophetic faith, compressing the radical significance of Israel's election into a terse summary of the theological basis of his message. Israel's election was the very reason for her punishment. God "watches over the established orders of international law," writes G. Von Rad (*Old Testament Theology*, vol. II, p. 135), "not only in Israel, but also among other nations, and whenever they are broken, He imposes a historical punishment upon the culprits. Israel's breaches are, of course, immeasurably more serious, since she was the nation with whom above all others He had made Himself intimate."

The prophet then proceeded to pose a series of questions, to which there could be only one reply. The illustrations were taken from everyday life and were used to emphasise that every event must have a cause, and if the prophet had spoken

as he had, there must have been an adequate cause which
impelled him to do so. The justification was implicit and his
authority plain.

TWO COMPANIONS
Do two walk together unless they have agreed? (3 : 3)

Those to whom Amos spoke were well aware of the dangers
of travelling in their day. No one would cross the hill country
by himself if he could possibly find a companion to go with
him. On the other hand, no one would travel with a stranger
whom he did not know and whose motives might be suspect.
If two men were seen walking together, it was a legitimate
assumption that they had arranged to meet and journey
together. In the lonely countryside they would not have met
by accident, but by appointment.

Amos had uttered what must have sounded startling statements and the people doubtless questioned his authority for
so doing. If he spoke the word of God, however, the prophet's
implicit claim was that he was walking in agreement with God.
He would not have acted on his own volition: his utterances
were due to a Divine and irresistible impulse.

The verse has, of course, often been used to teach the lesson
that none can live or work together unless they are at harmony
with each other, and that no marriage partners can expect
marital happiness if both are not believers. This is quite a
legitimate application, but Amos was referring primarily to
the question of cause and effect. If he spoke, it was only
because there was a cause—the impelling force of Jehovah
Himself.

THE HUNGRY LION
*Does a lion roar in the forest when he has no prey? Does
a young lion growl from his lair if he has taken nothing?
(3 : 4).*

As the listeners well knew, the lion's roar was never heard
in the silence of the desert before he had captured his prey.
He stalked his quarry silently, cautious lest the slightest sound

should alert it. Not until he sprang upon his prey was the ominous roar heard. The sound was the indication that he had made his capture. Similarly, declared Amos, the young lion never growled in satisfaction before food was brought to him. When he was tearing the carcase in his lair, his growls would be heard. In both cases, the sound indicated that something had happened. The sounds were the result of a cause.

So also the prophet's announcement of judgment did not spring from a frenzied imagination nor from a momentary personal impulse. He had declared the intentions of Jehovah, and since the sentence had been pronounced, the people must realise that he had spoken at the bidding of Jehovah and had been impelled to do so by the realisation of the urgency of the whole matter.

THE TRAPPED BIRD

Does a bird fall into a net on the ground when there is no bait for it? Does a snare spring up from the ground when it has taken nothing? (3 : 5).

Turning from the forest to the field, the prophet asked whether a bird was caught in a net without bait having been laid, or whether a trap was sprung if there was nothing there. It was the practice to stretch a net on the ground over two flaps. When the bait placed in the centre was seized by the bird, the flaps would spring up and trap the bird. It was obvious that a bird would not be caught in a net if there was no bait laid for it, and equally that the flaps of the trap would not spring up unless a bird had been caught.

Keil suggests that the prophet was virtually posing two other questions to his hearers; first, whether destruction could overtake the people if their sin did not draw them into it; and second, whether they could expect to escape the destruction without injury. Amos may, however, have been emphasising that the statements he had made of Jehovah's purpose were an indication that the snare was laid and that presently the spring would snap and they would be taken.

When punishment came, it would not be without cause; their own iniquities had formed the reason.

THE TRUMPET BLAST

Is a trumpet blown in a city, and the people are not afraid? Does evil befall a city if Jehovah has not done it? (3 : 6).

When the blast of a trumpet (*shophar*, horn) resounded through a city, the inhabitants would immediately be aware that the sentinel, who had sounded it, had perceived potential danger in the distance. His trumpet blast was a warning to the people to prepare for possible attack. Naturally the citizens would be disturbed by the sound. The prophet's warnings of impending trouble ought similarly to have shaken the people of Israel out of their sense of complacency and security and made them realise that danger was ahead.

If disaster of some kind befell a city, Israel concluded that it had some cause in the Divine purpose (cf. 1 Sam. 6 : 9). There might be some physical antecedent which gave rise to the calamity, but the Hebrews attributed the ultimate misfortune (such as famine or plague) to the hand of Jehovah, and He acted in this way because there was a cause—possibly in the character or conduct of those who thus suffered. If disaster was about to fall upon Israel, therefore, as Amos had clearly predicted, it was impossible for them to regard it in any other way than the working of God—and for some specific reason.

DIVINE REVELATION

For Adonai Jehovah does nothing except he reveals his secret to his servants the prophets. The lion has roared: who will not fear? Adonai Jehovah has spoken; who can but prophesy? (3 : 7, 8).

Commenting on verse 7, H. L. Ellison (*The Prophets of Israel, p. 79*) says that "the vital principle is that all God's acts among men reveal and are intended to reveal His character and will. It should stand to reason, therefore, that God will not leave Himself without men able to intepret those actions."

So far as Israel was concerned, before God took any important action in relation to the nation, He sent a messenger to disclose His intention and to warn or counsel the people on the attitude to take. He imparted a knowledge of His will and purposes to His servants (Jer. 23 : 18, 22). The people ought, therefore, to infer that Amos had stood in the Divine council and had been enlightened regarding the Divine policy: they ought consequently to take heed and obey.

People feared at the roar of the lion, but Amos had heard the voice of Jehovah the Sovereign. He had no alternative but to speak. He knew the horrors to come: he was compelled to prophesy. Is there not a message here for God's servants today? His voice was heard clearly and unmistakably at Calvary. He spoke: can any refrain from prophesying? He has revealed the judgment which lies ahead. Can we be dumb in view of the dangers confronting a guilty world? The preacher's voice should ring out with power and assurance. God has spoken: who can but prophesy?

Verse 8 has sometimes been connected with ch. 1 : 1, 2 with the suggestion that ch. 3 : 8 refers to the earthquake and the roar of Jehovah mentioned in the earlier passage. This is an interesting speculation, but it has little foundation.

THE SPECTATORS SUMMONED

Proclaim in the strongholds in Ashdod and in the strongholds in the land of Egypt and say, Assemble yourselves on the mountains of Samaria and see the great tumults in its midst and the oppression in its midst. They know not how to do right, says Jehovah, who store up violence and robbery in their strongholds (3 : 9, 10).

The city of Samaria was built on a hill some 300 feet high and was almost surrounded by mountains which were much higher and from these it was possible to look into the city and watch its busy streets and traffic. No walls surrounded the city, which formed an impressive crown to the hill (Isa. 28 : 1, 3), the mountains around making a natural amphitheatre.

The prophet called to the inhabitants of Ashdod and Egypt to assemble on the mountains of Samaria as spectators of what was happening in the city. (The LXX substitutes "the provinces of Assyria" and "the regions of Egypt" for "the strongholds in Ashdod" and "the strongholds in the land of Egypt." The R.S.V. also substitutes "Assyria" for "Ashdod"). The dramatic introduction to his message would naturally ensure a hearing for the prophet.

If Assyria and Egypt knew something of disorders and dissolute conduct, of violence and oppression, they were now invited to gaze upon the capital of a nation in which malpractices and corruption, tumult and confusion were, in the eyes of Amos, evidently unparalleled. They were to behold people who had lost all consciousness of righteousness and had become incapable of doing what was right. Moral standards had disappeared and justice was inoperative. Possessions unscrupulously amassed were stored in Samaria's strongholds.

Amos called upon the spectators to see the deplorable condition as though it was even more reprehensible than what had been condemned in their own countries. They were also to hear the fate of this wretched people, and presumably to learn thereby that there is a God in heaven who has authority over the kingdoms of men.

INVASION THREATENED

Therefore, thus says Adonai Jehovah, An adversary shall surround the land, and he shall bring down your strength from you, and your strongholds shall be pillaged (3 : 11).

Before the imaginary spectators whom Amos had figuratively summoned to Samaria, the Sovereign of the universe pronounced the fate of the guilty nation. He chose to inflict the well-deserved punishment by using another nation as His instrument. This did not imply approval of the character of the instrument: in His sovereignty the Almighty uses whomsoever He will. Even the ungodly are sometimes used to inflict chastisement upon the godly. In the case of Job, for example, He even used the devil as His instrument.

An adversary was to surround the land of Israel. There was no invader in prospect at the time of the prophecy and the people may well have argued that, if such an event was to occur, it could obviously be relegated to the distant future, but that argument would have been fallacious, as history indicates. The oppressive upper class of Israel had spoiled and robbed their own fellow-countrymen, who had been unable to defend themselves. They had oppressed the poor and defrauded them of their possessions. Now they would be completely recompensed for their misdeeds. Retribution would be exacted to the full.

Their strength would be brought down. Their physical defences would be destroyed: the impregnable fortresses would be battered down, the treasuries in which their stolen possessions had been stored would be pillaged, and the loot they had themselves accumulated would be plundered.

It all seemed highly improbable at the time. Israel was at peace; no foe threatened her; her wealthy oppressors were secure and no one could do them harm. Yet within the lifetime of some then living, the predicted blow fell. For three years Samaria was invested by the Assyrians. Then its buildings were shattered, its riches plundered, and many of those who continued to perpetuate the deeds of their fathers were carried away captive, while the power of Israel was broken for centuries.

THE REMNANT

Thus says Jehovah, As the shepherd rescues from the mouth of the lion two legs or a piece of an ear, so shall the people of Israel be rescued, who dwell in Samaria on the corner of a couch and on a damask divan (3 : 12).

As a shepherd, Amos knew from experience that a sheep was often caught by a wild animal and that the shepherd was accountable to the owner for any loss incurred. If an animal was, therefore, carried off, he would seek to recover some part or parts as evidence of the truth of his story. It might be only a couple of shinbones or an ear lappet, but that would suffice to prove that he had not sold the sheep to another person, and would relieve him of the necessity of paying the value of the sheep to the owner of the flock. The same provision appeared in the code of Hammurabi.

Israel was to be swept away by the invader in just punishment for her crimes. Yet Jehovah declared that a remnant would be delivered. He used the same example as a shepherd would. Two legs or a piece of an ear would be rescued—a small part of the whole nation and, by the very illustration, a part which had been mauled by the foe. Rescue had come almost too late, and the condition of the remnant was evidence of the suffering inflicted upon the nation.

The average Israelite would be content to wrap himself in his cloak and lie on the ground for his rest. But Amos depicted the luxury of those who dwelt at Samaria. There were there comfortable couches and soft divans with their silken cushions, upon which the wealthy would loll. All that would soon be a thing of the past. The cry of the oppressed had reached the ear of the Almighty and He was about to pour out His wrath upon those who so completely ignored the spiritual requirements of the law.

DIVINE VISITATION

Hear and testify against the house of Jacob, says Adonai Jehovah, Elohim of Sabaoth, that on the day I punish Israel for his transgressions, I will also punish the altars of Bethel, and the horns of the altar shall be cut off and fall to the ground. And I will smite the winter house with the summer house; and the houses of ivory shall perish, and many houses shall come to an end, says Jehovah (3 : 13-15).

Still addressing the imaginary spectators upon the mountains surrounding Samaria, as though they were observing the whole of the events concerning Israel's end, God called upon them to act as witnesses in the legal proceedings He was instituting against His people. He referred to the latter as the house of Jacob, thereby implying that all twelve tribes were still regarded in His eyes as one nation.

Jehovah described Himself as the Sovereign, the God of hosts. His summons to the heathen was a bitter humiliation to the proud nation which regarded itself as superior to all nations of the earth, but the crowning degradation was the exposure to the heathen of their condemnation and forthcoming fate.

Punishment was to fall, not merely upon Israel for their transgressions, but upon the very centre of their religion. This must have seemed inevitable. The people meticulously observed the ceremonial requirements of the law; they regularly presented their sacrifices and brought their tithes; they attended the set festivals; they engaged in religious pilgrimages. But Jehovah threatened judgment upon the altars of Bethel, indicating quite clearly His rejection of the whole system.

Bethel was the most popular sanctuary in Israel. It had been sanctified originally by Jeroboam I, but it had evidently been enlarged by his successors, its single altar had been replaced by a number, and a temple had been erected, the courts of which were apparently crowded with worshippers. Even if it was a schismatic site, the worship was still of Jehovah, in imitation of that at Jerusalem.

Like the altar at Jerusalem, that at Bethel was constructed with horns a cubit high at the corners. To these the sacrifices were bound, but they were also regarded as a protection of fugitives (1 Kings 1 : 50). Once the individual had caught hold of the horns of the altar, he deemed himself safe from his pursuer. Jehovah now announced that punishment was to fall upon the altar and that its horns would be cut off and fall to the ground. The falsity of the whole system was exposed and condemned but, in addition, the very protection extended by the altar was to be destroyed. Israel was to find no sanctuary in the hour of need, no refuge from the enemy who were soon to assail her.

The sanctuary of Bethel and its altar were eventually

destroyed by Josiah and the whole, including the high place and a neighbouring grove, were burned and then ground to powder (2 Kings 23 : 15).

The wealthy of Israel built themselves residences for winter and summer. They decorated some of their mansions with ivory (cf. 1 Kings 22 : 39). They lived luxuriously at the expense of the poor whom they had ground down. They gloried in their opulence and the comfort they enjoyed. The One, who saw their obsession with the material things of life and the unreality of all their religious professions, declared that He would smite their magnificent residences and bring to an end their houses of ivory and that, in fact, many mansions should be destroyed. This was, of course, completely fulfilled during the Assyrian invasion, although some commentators have suggested that destruction by earthquake may have occurred previously. There is, however, no historical record of this.

The first of the three discourses ended with a picture of destruction and desolation, God had spoken clearly and unmistakenly.

CHAPTER 6

The Second Discourse

IN the first discourse, Amos virtually presented his credentials and argued that he had spoken only because of God's impulse: that there was always a cause for every effect. In the second discourse, he described the methods already employed by God in the attempt to secure the people's repentance and return to Himself, as well as some of the methods about to be employed. He commenced with what has been justifiably called his bitterest oracle, which was directed against the pampered ladies of Israel.

KINE OF BASHAN

Hear this word, you cows of Bashan, who are in the mountain of Samaria, who oppress the poor, who crush the needy, who say to their husbands, Bring and let us drink. Adonai Jehovah has sworn by his holiness that, lo, days are coming upon you when they will take you away with hooks and the last of you with fish-hooks. And you shall go out through the breaches, every one straight before her, and you shall be cast into Harmon, says Jehovah (4: 1-3).

The luxury and self-indulgence of the affluent in Israel was in stark contrast to the plight of the impecunious peasant and artisan. It was all the more scandalous because the wealth of the privileged classes had been wrung from the poor. Amos disclosed that the oppression of the working class and the crushing of the afflicted were not due entirely to the calculated cupidity of the men who were responsible for their sufferings.

The instigation came from petulant selfishness of their wives. "All the Hebrew prophets," writes J. E. McFadyen (*A Cry for Justice,* p. 36), "know that for the temper and quality of a civilisation the women are greatly responsible."

The prophet described these sleek, well-fed women, who spent their days in voluptuous dalliance or indolent *ennui,* as cows of Bashan, who lived in the hill country of Samaria. Bashan was noted for the excellence of its cattle: its rich pastures in the east of Jordan produced the fattest and strongest animals (Deut. 32 : 24; Psa. 22 : 12), and they were used as a symbol of the mighty (Ezek. 39 : 18). It was an appropriate simile for these female sybarites, whose hedonism was apparent to all.

They cared nothing for the price paid for their pleasure: all they sought was the gratification of their passing whims. It mattered nothing to them—even if they were aware of it— that their "luxuries were continually watered by tears of the poor." They constantly demanded more from their husbands that their desires might be satiated. To meet their demands meant further oppression of the poor and even trampling upon the needy, but provided their husbands were able to extort what they wanted, they were not concerned about the odious practices which were necessary. It was because of their action —which drove the men to exercise even greater pressure on the suffering poor—that Amos justifiably accused them of the wrongs and injustices perpetrated to supply their demands. But these wantons were indifferent to the woes of others.

The Lord God had sworn by His holiness that retribution should come to these "kine of Bashan". The seriousness of the oath marked the fixed determination of the Almighty. They would be dragged away with hooks and the last of them (possibly their back parts) with fish-hooks. Suddenly and unexpectedly they would meet their fate. God's indignation at their attitude could be satisfied only by their suffering for their evil-doing. The disdainful creatures were to be dragged out of their comfort and luxury, to exchange their lot for wretched slavery. The reference to hooks may have been intended quite literally, for the Assyrian monuments show the captives being dragged off with hooks in their mouths. The humiliation and indignity were all the greater because of their previous privileged position.

Through the breaches made in the walls by the enemy, the captives would pass in a long line, tormented by the hooks in their mouths or noses. Each would follow straight on, not looking now, as hitherto, for the crowd to gaze upon her finery, but in shame at her condition and semi-nudity, like a herd of cows they pass through the holes in the walls to be "cast forth in Harmon". The location of Harmon is not known. The Peshitta identifies it as "the mountain of Armenia" and Jerome also gave this interpretation. The Septuagint substitutes the Romman (or Rhomman) mountain. Others have translated the word Rimmon, the Syrian goddess of love, and have assumed that the women were handed over to be used as prostitutes in the temple of the goddess.

The LXX translation implies that the humbling of the women commenced immediately, for it reads, "you shall be dragged out naked over against one another and cast naked on Romman mountain". Some commentators assume that the whole of the women were to be slain and cast out as corpses, but this would be inconsistent with the customary practice. Normally the women would be the prey of the conquering army and would suffer a terrible fate at the hand of the soldiers and probably be used later in prostitution in the temples. This is evidently what actually happened. Their disregard for the sufferings of others was amply repaid in that day.

LIFELESS RELIGION

Come to Bethel and transgress, to Gilgal and multiply transgressions; bring your sacrifices every morning, and your tithes every three days. Offer a thank-offering sacrifice of that which is leavened, and proclaim freewill offerings: publish them, for this pleases you, O you people of Israel, says Adonai Jehovah (4: 4, 5)

"It is a characteristic of idolatry and schism," wrote Wordsworth long ago, "to profess extraordinary zeal for God's worship and go beyond the letter and spirit of His law by arbitrary will-worship and self-idolising fanaticism." This was particularly relevant to the people of Israel at this time. Despite the social injustices and oppression for which they were responsible, they scrupulously observed all the ritual of religion and even went beyond the specific requirements of the law. It was as though they deemed this an adequate compensation for their inconsistency of life and an automatic guarantee of their acceptance by God. The lack of moral and practical conformity to the will of God did not seem to concern them.

In an ironical exhortation to the worshippers at Israel's shrines, Jehovah tore away the rags of their false pretensions and hypocritical posturings and revealed His contempt for their insincerity and unreality. He did not condemn their schismatic sanctuaries or their man-made priesthood, their choice of Bethel and Gilgal in place of Jerusalem. These were only symptomatic of the more deep-seated evil of their hearts.

Bethel had been set apart as a religious centre by Jeroboam I and was regarded as a royal sanctuary and a royal court (Am. 7: 13). Gilgal, near Shechem, had not the special character of Bethel, but it was the first place at which the people had camped in Canaan after crossing the Jordan and Joshua had erected a stone cairn there (Josh. 4 : 19, 20). It was there that circumcision again took place as a reminder of Israel's separation from other nations to God (Josh. 5 : 2, 9). It was here that Saul, the first king of Israel, was crowned (1 Sam. 11 : 14, 15). Altars had been erected at Gilgal and offerings were presented there (Hos. 12 : 11). Both Bethel and Gilgal were sites at which Jehovah was allegedly worshipped.

Quite apart from the fact that the sites were not the divinely appointed one at Jerusalem, how could God accept the offerings of such as Israel. He rejected their pious practices. Parodying ecclesiastical language, He ironically called upon them to come to Bethel—not to worship but to transgress— and to come to Gilgal to multiply their transgressions. At the very time when the people were offering sacrifices to God in a punctilious performance of all the rites and ceremonies of the temple, they were still engaging in social malpractices. Their piety was intolerable. It was an externalism of unspiritual ritualists.

There was no consciousness of guilt on the part of these zealous religionists. No sin or trespass offerings were apparently offered: they were deemed superfluous. But they brought their burnt offerings, peace offerings and freewill offerings. These they presented daily, as though the very frequency might secure greater favour with God.

The law required the rendering of tithes annually and the second tithe triennially (Deut. 14 : 28), but God called them in mockery to present their tithes every three days. They brought their peace offerings but apparently sacrificed by fire their leavened bread, which was not to be offered on the altar but presented with the sacrifice (Lev. 7 : 14). By sacrificing leaven to God they were infringing His commandment and virtually insulting Him.

Jehovah bade them proclaim their freewill offerings, but this flamboyant proclamation could only be for self-glorification. Publicise them, He told them, because this was what they loved to do. In their self-righteousness, it pleased them to carry out the ritual of worship, but to advertise what they were doing brought even greater pleasure to them. The Divine voice bade them carry on in what was no more than spiritual rebellion. Of what value were such offerings from men whose conduct was so reprehensible?

They are not without their disciples today. There are those whose conduct and behaviour are far from God-honouring, but who are prepared to boast of what they do in the service of Christ—as though the most that man could ever do could make our Lord in the slightest degree his debtor. God has no place for unreality and insincerity.

FAMINE

I gave you cleanness of teeth in all your cities and lack of bread in all your places. Yet you did not return to me, says Jehovah (4 : 6).

In verses 6 to 11 are detailed catastrophes which God brought upon Israel, with the specific object of arousing them to a realisation of their dependence upon Him, and of the sin which had caused the withdrawal of His benefits from them. Yet they were quite oblivious to their need and to His message. The five calamities were: famine (v. 6), drought (vv. 7, 8), crop failure (v. 9), pestilence (v. 10) and earthquake (v. 11). Each of the statements ended with the expression, "Yet you did not return to me."

The first example given of Jehovah's providential dealings was the infliction of famine. Picturesquely He said that He had given them cleanness of teeth and lack of bread in city and country. There could be no dubiety about the significance of the famine. Israel knew perfectly well that this was one of the means Divinely employed to chastise them for wrongdoing. As one writer says, it was "the implementation of curses for breach of covenant obligations." It would have been a foolish man who claimed that what had happened was merely a natural occurrence. Yet the punitive hand of the Almighty had no effect upon the attitude of His people.

DROUGHT

And I also withheld the rain from you when there were yet three months to harvest: and I would send rain on one city and would send no rain on another city. One portion of land would be rained upon, and the portion of land on which it did not rain withered. So two or three cities would wander to another city to drink water, but they would not be satisfied. Yet you did not return to me, says Jehovah (4 : 7, 8).

Rain at the right periods of the year is an inestimable blessing in the east. The people of Israel would regard it as the gift of God. When it fell, it was a sign of His blessing. When it was withheld, it was an indication of His displeasure. Over a long period, Jehovah had evidently employed this means of convicting His wayward people, but they continued to ignore the lesson.

The reference is to the heavy winter rains, which came from October to February. These were followed in March and April by the "latter rain". The heavy winter rains had been withheld, so that the May harvest was doomed. God demonstrated that it was His act by causing rain to fall upon one field but not another, with the result that the latter withered. There could be no doubt, but the people completely ignored what was happening.

They tottered from one city to another, only to find that the underground cisterns of the more fortunate cities had an inadequate supply to meet the needs of others as well and they were left unsatisfied. Yet, despite their need, they did not return to Jehovah.

CROP FAILURE

I smote you with blight and mildew. I laid waste your gardens and your vineyards. When your fig trees and olive trees increased, the locust devoured them. Yet you did not return to me, says Jehovah (4 : 9).

One of the curses threatened if Israel did not obey Jehovah was blight and mildew (Deut. 28 : 22). As in the other catastrophes, therefore, they should plainly have recognised this as the hand of God when the infliction came. He declared that He smote them with blight and mildew, ravaged their gardens and vineyards and destroyed their figs and olives by the locust. Famine and drought had been ignored; surely this sweeping calamity of the fields would draw them back in penitence to Him.

The blight was caused by the blasting east winds and the mildew by a combination of heat and damp. The locust (the *gazam* or shearer) was a frequent cause of trouble in Palestine and the swarms would eat every green thing. Yet, despite all the loss involved, the people still did not return to Jehovah.

PESTILENCE

I sent among you a pestilence after the manner of Egypt. I slew your young men with the sword and carried away your horses. And I made the stench of your camp come up to your nostrils. Yet you did not return to me, says Jehovah (4 : 10).

Pestilence was also detailed in the law as one of the judgments of God (Deut. 28 : 21). For Israel's transgressions, Jehovah had sent an epidemic among them, which he likened to that of Egypt. This probably does not refer to a plague which was peculiar to that country, but rather to the fact that Egypt was subject to epidemics and that Israel was to suffer as Egyptians frequently did. Pliny says that Egypt was the mother of contagious diseases.

At the same time there had been military conflict and many of the young men had been slain and their horses carried away by the victors. Their corpses evidently lay unburied and the sickening stench of the decaying bodies filled the air and probably contributed to the effects of the pestilence. Once again, it might have been anticipated that the blow would cause people to turn in contrition to Jehovah. Yet they did not return.

EARTHQUAKE

I overthrew some of you, as Elohim overthrew Sodom and Gomorrah, and you were as a brand plucked out of the fire. Yet you did not return to me, says Jehovah (4 : 11).

The last of the five punitive actions described was an earthquake, comparable to the one which destroyed Sodom and Gomorrah (Gen. 19 : 24, 25)—possibly the one referred to in ch. 1 : 1. The cities were blotted out because of their gross sin and immorality. It was but just that Israel should suffer in similar fashion for her transgressions. The earthquake was perhaps the most fearful visitation imaginable and was God's final attempt to carry conviction home to the people.

Nevertheless, mercy preserved some. Not all were destroyed. The survivors were like a brand plucked out of the fire, delivered not so much by their own efforts as by the compassion of Jehovah. Surely this last experience would bring a realisation of their guilt to the remnant left. Yet they did not return to God. The nation was completely incorrigible.

FINAL WARNING

Therefore, thus will I do to you, O Israel. Because I will do this to you, prepare to meet your God, O Israel. For, lo, he who forms the mountains and creates the wind, and reveals to man what his meditation is, who makes dawn darkness, and treads on the heights of the earth, Jehovah, Elohim of Sabaoth, is his name (4 : 12, 13).

After all His providential dealings with His people, which had proved completely ineffective in arresting them or attracting them back to Himself, Jehovah issued a final warning. He had detailed the scourges which had successively fallen upon Israel and the listeners must have envisioned Him with hand uplifted to strike the last blow. His words did imply a judicial act, "thus will I do to you," but He gave no details of what was about to occur. Some expositors not unnaturally consider that the words implied the judgment of a future day —possibly the great tribulation of which our Lord subsequently spoke (Matt. 24 : 21), or alternatively the final assize of Rev. 20 : 11-15. The text, however, gives no indication of the character of the action threatened. We are not told what the disaster was to be.

In the light of it, however, Jehovah called upon Israel to prepare to meet their God. It is not clear that the words precluded any possibility of national or personal repentance, as is commonly assumed. They may have been intended to offer a last opportunity for an amendment of attitude and ways. Even at that stage, the sentence might at least be mitigated.

"Prepare to meet your God." The words have arrested many an individual since and awakened him to a realisation of the danger in which he stood. But they were words addressed to God's covenant nation, and words which have relevance to His people today. Many a believer is utterly complacent about his position: his future is assured and no perturbation affects him. He is indifferent to the needs of the whole world around and equally indifferent to the unsanctified character of his own life. There is a need for the constant reminder that we may soon meet the One to whom an account must be rendered and that, at the judgment seat of Christ (2 Cor. 5 : 10), the whole of our life and service will be brought under review.

It is claimed that verse 13 is a hymn and that Amos contains two others (5 : 8, 9; 9 : 5, 6), each of them being a self-delineation of Jehovah. It does at least describe the power and might of the One who had spoken so plainly to Israel and the description follows logically upon the final warning of verse 12. This was the God whom Israel had to meet.

The mighty Creator, by whom not only mountains but all things came into existence, the origin of spirit and health, declared that His meditation or plan was revealed to man. He unveiled Himself and disclosed His purposes that man might understand. However true that was in the days of Amos, it is a far clearer fact today. The full and complete revelation of God, His character and purposes, has been made in the Person of Christ. He is God's final word to man.

He stated also that He made dawn darkness and trod on the heights of the earth. These were pictorial indications of an approaching thunder-storm. The clear sky suddenly darkened as the masses of storm clouds collected. The rolling thunder reverberated over the hills and mountains as though some mighty being was traversing the heights of the earth. The freshening wind acted as a warning precursor. The lightning flash revealed the form of the mountains through the clouds. The LXX indeed substitutes "thunder" for "mountains" in the first clause of verse 13.

It was a popular view among the Hebrews that a thunderstorm marked the presence of God and it was, therefore, appropriate that He should describe in this fearful way the One whom Israel was to prepare to meet.

CHAPTER 7

The Third Discourse

THE third of the three major discourses delivered by Amos commenced with a dirge to be sung at the funeral of the ailing nation of Israel and visualised her decease as having already occurred. The significance must have dawned upon the prophet's hearers and it was doubtless one of the contributory factors to the growing resentment, which burst out later through the high priest of Bethel (7 : 12). The discourse naturally went farther and probed the conduct of the people still further.

THE DIRGE

Hear this word which I take up over you in lamentation, O house of Israel. The virgin of Israel is fallen: she will rise no more. She is cast down on her land, none to raise her up. For thus says Adonai Jehovah, The city that went out a thousand shall have a hundred left, and that which went forth a hundred shall have ten left, to the house of Israel (5 : 1-3).

In his previous discourse the prophet had called upon the nation to prepare to meet their God, and the whole tenor of his statements was that, whatever means Jehovah had used, the people remained unwilling to turn in contrition to Him, and that judgment, therefore, was inevitable. He now gave voice to his lamentation as though the judgment had fallen and the dead body of Israel lay before him. He regarded the predicted events as a *fait accompli*, so that it was time for the final obsequies to take place. Hence his funeral dirge.

Those over whom he mourned were doubtless full of good spirits and natural buoyancy, but Amos was more farseeing than they.

A dirge, says Driver (*ibid*, p. 175), was "not a spontaneous effusion of natural emotion, but a composition, longer or shorter as the case may be, constructed with some art in a definite poetical form, and chanted usually by women, whose profession it was to attend mourning ceremonies for the purpose." Amos called upon no professional mourners. He uttered the dirge himself: if tears were shed, they were his alone.

His lamentation was not the usual elaborate and flowery poetry common at his time, but a very brief and concise statement by the prophet as chief mourner. No relations and friends joined him in the expression of grief, as was usual. Israel was at its zenith of power and prosperity: how could these people believe that their downfall was imminent?

Amos personified the nation as a virgin maid—an indirect reference to the fact that Israel was still an unconquered and independent nation. But, in the prophet's eyes, the virgin lay prostrate on the ground, violated by the savage foe and abandoned to her fate. The blithe and carefree nation had been ravaged and brutally maltreated, he declared (as, in fact, was to happen at a later date, to which his words really referred). No more would she arise; there was no one to raise her up. Her doom was sealed and her condition was hopeless.

When the day came which he envisaged, Israel's military forces would be decimated. A city might send out a thousand, but only a hundred would return. Another might equip a hundred, but ninety would lose their lives. The language might be picturesque, but he was describing what was actually to occur. Well might the funeral dirge resound through the land already. Doom and destruction could no longer be averted.

SEEK THE LORD

For thus says Jehovah to the house of Israel, Seek me and

you shall live. But do not seek Bethel and do not enter into Gilgal nor cross over to Beersheba: for Gilgal shall surely go into captivity and Bethel shall come to nothing. Seek Jehovah and live, lest he break out like fire in the house of Joseph and destroy it and there be none to quench it for Bethel (5 : 4-6).

Israel's doom had been announced, yet Jehovah still offered a way of escape. If they would only seek Him (and implicitly make this the habitual attitude of life) and forsake their idolatry and their evil ways, they would live. This was not an appeal for an emotional and temporary change of heart. What God sought was tantamount to a complete transformation of purpose and outlook. Schmoller (Lange's *Commentary*, p. 37) pertinently remarks, "Only he, therefore, seeks the Lord in truth, who seeks good, and vice versa. And this seeking of good is more closely defined as hating evil and loving good. Both must concur . . . Evil must be earnestly repelled and shunned, otherwise the seeking of good lacks truth and energy; in like manner must good be grasped at, otherwise the attempt misses the aim and soon becomes fruitless. Piety must have an ethical element, must show itself by hating evil and loving good. A mere outward religiousness, however zealous in ceremonies, is worthless in the eyes of God." This was the crux of the matter: there must be a change of heart.

We need the same reminder today. The sloppy sentimentality of the gospel appeal of a decade or two ago to "Come to Jesus" was a gross misrepresentation of the call of God. What the sinner needs is a realisation of the heinousness of his sin and the gravity of his condition and a clear challenge to leave his evil ways and to accept a new life in Christ. He cannot seek God unless he is prepared to turn his back on his sins.

Even more fallacious and misleading, of course, is the current appeal to love one another and to "love Jesus". This is not the answer to human need. There is no acknowledgment here of the depravity of the human heart. How can an unregenerate sinner love God or his fellow-men? The whole concept is an insult to human intelligence. Before we can love God or others, there must be a personal regeneration, a complete change of heart. Sin must be eschewed and a new outlook be allowed to spring from a new nature.

Do not seek to Bethel or Gilgal or cross over the frontier to Beersheba, besought the prophet. This would be utter folly. In any case, they were schismatic centres already under the Divine curse. Whatever their traditional associations, these illegal sites could not meet the present need of the Israelite. Gilgal was condemned: it should go into captivity. There was a play on words here which George Adam Smith shows more clearly in his rendering, "Gilgal shall taste the gall of exile." Bethel (literally "the house of God") should become Aven, or "vanity". Since these sanctuaries were rejected by Jehovah, of what use was it to resort to them?

With additional emphasis and an implication of urgency, the prophet again exhorted the people to seek Jehovah and live. This was their only way of escape. Jehovah was about to burst out like fire in the house of Joseph, i.e., the northern kingdom of Israel, and to destroy it. Once that fire was kindled, nothing could extinguish it. Bethel would be consumed by it. God's wrath was often depicted in the O.T. as a fire (Deut. 4 : 24; Jer. 4 : 4). He might use others as His instruments—as, of course, He did in the case of Israel—but the origin of the destruction was Jehovah Himself. The people were, therefore, faced with the choice. Either they could repent of their wickedness and turn to God, or they must face the consequences of their rejection.

GOD OF THE HEAVENS

You who turn justice to wormwood and cast down righteousness to the earth, seek him who made the Pleiades and Orion, and turns the shadow of death into the morning, and darkens the day into night: who calls the waters of the sea and pours them out on the face of the earth—Jehovah is his name—who causes destruction to flash forth against the strong, so that destruction comes upon the fortress (5 : 7-9).

Addressing primarily the wealthy merchants of Israel who had established themselves by oppression of the poor, the prophet declared that they turned justice to wormwood and cast down righteousness to the earth. Wormwood was a plant with an extremely bitter taste (Deut. 29 : 18) and it was frequently used as a symbol of bitter experience or calamity (Jer. 23 : 15). The accusation was that justice in the courts had been so perverted that it was bitterness to those who suffered. If the rich could secure his end in no other way, he bribed the judge to obtain a favourable verdict. A poor man had little prospect of a fair or favourable ruling. Justice was synonymous with bitterness. Instead of maintaining a standard of righteousness, it was hurled to the ground. Right was defeated by might or money.

Yet even to men such as these, the prophet appealed to seek Jehovah. He proceeded to describe the power and might of that One. He was the maker of Pleiades and Orion and, by inference, if such conspicuous constellations owed their existence to Him, the whole of the starry heavens must have been the work of His hand. He was, moreover, the One who ordered the regular alternation of day and night. He dispersed the darkness of night, "the shadow of death", with the roseate hues of the dawn, and He plunged the evening of the day into sudden darkness. He was, in addition, the One who raised the waters of the sea by evaporation to the clouds above and then, in due course, poured them out again as rain upon the face of the earth. This was the covenant God of Israel. Jehovah was His name.

Keil (*ibid*, p. 281) takes a typological glance at the phrases of verse 8. He says, "As the Almighty turns the darkness of death into light, and the deepest misery into prosperity and health, so He darkens the bright day of prosperity into the dark night of adversity, and calls to the waters of the sea to force themselves over the earth like the flood, and destroy the ungodly."

It was God, declared Amos, who caused destruction to break forth upon the strong so that the fortress was destroyed. It is probable that what was envisaged was the military attack which would break the defences of Israel and overcome the mighty warriors and ultimately destroy their fortifications. J. B. Taylor (*The Minor Prophets*, p. 34) interestingly suggests that "verse 9 almost certainly conceals the names of three further constellations, Taurus (the Bull), Capricornus (the Goat) and Vindemiator (the Grape-gatherer), but these were not recognised by the Massoretes who inserted the vowel-points, so we have to translate them by "destruction", "the strong" and "the fortress". This seems more consistent with the context.

MONITOR AT THE GATE

They hate him who reproves in the gate, and they abhor him who speaks the truth (5 : 10).

In the cities and large villages, justice was administered in the gateway, along the walls of which the elders or judges sat to hear cases and to give their decisions. The proceedings were not so formal as in the west, and often all the adult male citizens would sit in solemn conclave. They heard disputes, tendered advice, acted as advocates or reconcilers and arbiters. In Israel at that time, according to Amos, they were unfortunately susceptible to bribery and persuasion by corrupt methods.

When a monitor or reprover rose up to object to an act of injustice or to an unjust assessment of a case, he naturally aroused the ire and antagonism of the wealthy citizens who had so lavishly bribed the court. When one insisted that what was right should be done and presented the true facts in the case, they were bitterly opposed to him. The prophet used strong words—"hate" and "abhor"—but they doubtless represented the actual attitude adopted.

THE OPPRESSORS' LOSS

Therefore, because you trample upon the poor and take from him exactions of wheat: you have built houses of hewn stone, but you shall not live in them; you have planted pleasant vineyards, but you shall not drink their wine. For I know how many are your transgressions and how great are your sins. You oppress the righteous, you take a bribe, and you turn aside the needy in the gate. Therefore, the prudent will keep silence at that time, for it is an evil time (5 : 11-13).

The avaricious urban class which had grown up had contrived, in many instances, to acquire the land of the small farmers by foreclosing mortgages, by dishonest business practices and by plain distortion. The unfortunate victims had then been placed in the unhappy position of having to pay a rental for their land, usually in the form of a levy of some kind upon the crops. Amos denounced the wealthy schemers for their oppression of the poor and for the toll of wheat they exacted as rental of the land they had improperly gained.

He declared that, with their ill-gotten gains, they had built for themselves houses of hewn stones (most houses being constructed of dried brick) and had planted pleasant vineyards for their enjoyment. But there was a righteous God in heaven. They might build, but they would never live in their luxurious mansions. They might plant, but they would never drink the wine produced in the vineyards. Their machinations would be of no value to them. All their schemes would come to nothing.

Jehovah declared that He knew how many were their transgressions and how great were their sins. They could not conceal their practices from Him. Their guilt was exposed. He cited three specific wrongs for which they were responsible, viz. (a) the oppression of the righteous, (b) the giving and accepting of bribes, and (c) the thwarting of the needy in the gate. All three were connected with the administration of justice. Mays (*ibid*, p. 97) pertinently writes, "For Amos the court in the gate is the central institution in Israel, and the integrity of the members of the legal assembly the most crucial issue of Jehovah's authority over society. He looks neither to the royal administration nor to the cult as the source and centre of righteousness and justice, but to the legal assembly in the villages."

In the giving of false evidence, in the deliberate corrupting of the judges, and in the frustration of the needy by turning him aside from his rights, the *nouveau riche* of Israel were destroying the very instrument by which God's justice was administered amongst His people. The crimes which were being committed had been strictly forbidden by the law (Exod. 23 : 1-8).

It was no wonder that the wise man, realising the futility and danger of trying to intervene, remained silent. He realised the evil character of the times. The malignity of opponents might matter little, but the moral corruption which was prevalent made it patent that it was too late to speak.

GOOD OR EVIL

Seek good and not evil, that you may live: and so Jehovah, the God of hosts, will be with you, as you have said. Hate evil and love good, and establish justice in the gate. It may be that Jehovah, God of hosts, will be gracious to the remnant of Joseph (5 : 14, 15).

The misguided in Israel prided themselves upon their covenant relationship with God. No evil could befall them because Jehovah was with them. They did not realise that their own inconsistency of necessity invoked punishment. They could not believe that God could turn against Israel.

Amos accordingly enjoined them again to turn their backs upon their sinful ways. Jehovah was aware of their true character and conduct. What fellowship could there be between light and darkness? "Seek good and not evil," he cried. This alone was the way of life. Continuance in their present practices would only remove them from Divine favour, but if they changed their attitude, Jehovah would certainly be with them, as they so often claimed He was.

They must, however, implement their intentions in a practical manner. Let them show by their conduct that they detested evil and loved good. The way of demonstrating this was to re-establish justice in the gate. If they swept away the vile system of false evidence, bribery and corruption, and insisted that only just decisions should be given, this would be an evidence of their change of heart. It was possible, in such circumstances, God would still be gracious to a remnant of them. The majority must pay the price, but some might even yet be delivered.

Is there not a message here for God's people today? The inconsistency and hypocrisy which are so widespread are known to God. He is aware of the true character and is not deceived by our false pretensions. If we still love our sins and indulge our desires in secret, how can we expect to escape His hand of chastisement? Our relationship to Him is no guarantee of immunity from punishment. Yet He still holds open the door for the erring one to return. But He seeks, not merely pious platitudes, but a change of heart and conduct, which prove the reality of the penitence.

UNIVERSAL WAILING

Therefore, thus says Jehovah, the God of hosts, Adonai, In all the squares there shall be wailing, and in all the streets they shall say, Alas! Alas! And they shall call the husbandman to mourning, and those who are skilled in lamentation to wailing. And in all vineyards there shall be wailing: for I will pass through the midst of you, says Jehovah (5 : 16, 17).

The obduracy of the oppressors could not be allowed to continue for ever unchecked, and Jehovah now predicted the fate that would befall them. The consequences were described before the cause was indicated. Death would be on every side: not one quarter would be exempt. The lamentations which were heard as the hired mourners wailed would resound through the city and country. In every broad place or square the loud cries would break out. In every street there would be the cry of woe as bereavement struck every home. Wailing would arise from the farm labourer and from the vinedresser. But ironically they would be called to participate in the funeral rites of those who had trodden them down.

Death had struck the land because Jehovah had passed through their midst. No longer could they avoid the penalty for their crimes against humanity or for their social injustices. The great Judge had taken account. Sentence had been passed and had now finally been executed.

Obviously instruments would have been used by Jehovah, but the agents were not described, but war, famine and pestilence, previously employed to accomplish the Divine purposes, were clearly the means used again in this case.

THE DAY OF THE LORD

Woe to you who desire the day of Jehovah! To what end is the day of Jehovah for you? It is darkness and not light. As if a man fled from a lion, and a bear met him; or went into his house and leaned his hand against the wall, and a serpent bit him. Is not the day of Jehovah darkness and not light? Even very dark and no brightness in it? (5 : 18-20).

"Time and again," writes R. Fey, "the Lord had sent His judgments upon His people in warning. . . . Yet Israel would not heed God's warning. With astonishing self-righteousness they even looked forward to 'the day of the Lord'. Were they not the chosen people? . . . 'The day of the Lord' would be a day of vindication and light. Their honour would be increased and their kingdom even more firmly established. Such was the optimism of the prosperous, who expected peace and glory apart from judgment. . . . Into the midst of this smug complacency Amos hurled his words of doom." This admirably sums up the sense of the next brief section of the prophecy.

The day of Jehovah is consistently described in the Old Testament as a period of judgment, with clouds and thick darkness. Yet these foolish people of Israel had expressed a longing for that day. Of what possible benefit could it be to them? The impression that it would bring blessing and deliverance from their foes, that it was a day of sunshine and rejoicing, was one which was quickly dispelled. It would be a day of darkness and not light, one which, in fact, was very dark and had no brightness at all. It would be a period of destruction, so their infatuated hopes should be dismissed.

Amos illustrated the character of the period from what was probably past experience of his herdman's life. The Israelite had expected salvation at that time: it would be more accurate to anticipate trouble. He pictured a man fleeing from a lion, only to be confronted by a bear—and the Syrian bear was fiercer than a lion. He imagined the fleeing man eventually reaching the security of his own home and leaning breathless and palpitating against the sunbaked brick wall of his house. But at the moment of relief, a snake's head suddenly protruded from a crack in the wall and the man's hand, resting against the wall, was bitten by the snake. The lesson was obvious and one which would be readily understood by those to whom the prophet spoke. There was no hope of salvation through Jehovah's intervention in that day. It was one of unmitigated judgment. Escape from one blow might only involve falling under another.

EMPTY RELIGION

I hate, I despise your festivals, and I will not smell the savour of your solemn assemblies. Even though you offer me your burnt offerings and your meal offerings, I will not accept them. Neither will I look on your peace offerings of fatted beasts. Take away from me the noise of your songs; for I will not listen to the melody of your harps (5 : 21-23).

Amos's listeners probably argued that the judgments he had predicted could not possibly fall upon them. Not only were they covenant people, but their religious worship must plainly bring satisfaction to God. It was their means of communion with Him, and all that was directed in the law was carried out at their sanctuaries. They observed the set festivals of the calendar, they presented their offerings and sacrifices, they chanted the praises of God; they were meticulous in the carrying out of all the rites and ceremonies.

To their utter amazement, Amos declared that God rejected their religious observances and practices *in toto*—festivals, sacrifices, and praise. They made their annual pilgrimages on the festival occasions—at the feast of unleavened bread, at Pentecost, and at the feast of tabernacles (Lev. 23)—but God declared that He completely rejected their festivals, that He hated and despised them.

They brought their burnt offerings and watched the entire animal consumed upon the altar as a sweet savour offering to God (Lev. 1 : 3-9) and as a symbol of their total commitment to Him. They presented their meal offerings and saw part consumed with the burnt offering (Lev. 2 : 1-3). They offered their peace offerings, a communion offering which the worshipper and the priest shared with Jehovah (Lev. 3 : 1-5). All that was sacrificed upon the altar was assumed to be of a sweet savour to Jehovah. But He declared His refusal to smell the savour, His rejection of the burnt and meal offerings and His unwillingness to look upon (or to participate in) the peace or communion offering. He could have no fellowship with such unworthy worshippers.

Their praises rang out to Him in their sacred sites and the temple choir chanted their songs to His glory, accompanying their singing with harps and other musical instruments, after the fashion of the choir at Jerusalem. Jehovah bade them to take away the hideous noise of their singing and closed His ears to the sound of their harps. Their religious services were an abomination to Him. They could not be accepted because of their unworthy conduct and their refusal to repent. Possibly, at the judgment seat of Christ, many believers of today will find their service rejected because of their inconsistency also.

JUSTICE AND RIGHTEOUSNESS

But let justice roll on like waters and righteousness as a perennial stream (5 : 24).

If their offerings and festivals were unacceptable, what could the people do? The prophet's reply was simple and direct. Justice had been evicted from her rightful place; righteousness had been driven from the court and the market-place. Let "justice roll on like waters and righteousness as an overflowing stream." If communion with God was to be restored, there must be a revival of justice and just dealings between man and man; injustices must be swept away; righteousness must replace the present oppressive and dishonest practices. The old standards must be re-erected, and social morality become not an icy principle but a warm, pulsating motivation of life.

Just as the waters flood down the wadi in the rainy season, and the perennial stream continues to flow in the driest of summers, so let justice and righteousness flow through court, market, home and business centre, flooding the whole scene with freshness and cleansing away every impurity. Thus alone could there be reconciliation to God.

J. E. McFadyen (in *A Cry for Justice*) says, "These are immortal words; they express in imperishable form the essence of religion, the simple demands of God upon man. The justice, the righteousness for which Amos here pleads is . . . a social thing: it is a tender regard for the poor, hatred of the evil conditions that have dwarfed their lives (5 : 15); it is the spirit that yearns and works for the removal of these conditions; it is, in a word, respect for personality, fair play as between man and man. Let justice, in that sense, run through society, unimpeded by avarice or selfishness or cruelty, let it roll on without let or hindrance like the waves of the sea; let it roll on unintermittently, all the year round, whatever be the political weather; let it roll on 'like a perennial stream', which even in the fiercest heat of summer never dries up."

TRUE OR FALSE
Did you bring to me sacrifices and offerings the forty years in the wilderness, O house of Israel? (5 : 25).

The people prided themselves on their fidelity to their religious system and persuaded themselves that their faithful carrying out of its rites and ceremonies guaranteed the favour of God and demonstrated their intimate relationship with Him. Jehovah had stated quite plainly that their religious observances meant nothing to Him. He did not criticise their golden calves or man-appointed priesthood, their false shrines or imitated festivals and sacrifices: He dismissed the whole as nauseating. It was the worthless system of a recreant race.

Were sacrifices and offerings essential to a relationship with Him? Micah states quite specifically that what God desires is not so much the sacrifice of animals as the practical righteousness of a life attuned to Him (Mic. 6 : 6-8). Jeremiah categorically declares that God gave no command regarding offerings and sacrifices at the exodus from Egypt, and that what He did command was obedience to His voice and walking in His ways.

"Did you bring me sacrifices and offerings the forty years in the wilderness?" He asked. The question may have one of two meanings: either that sacrifices were unnecessary to establish communion with God, or that the people failed to fulfil their obligations to offer sacrifices during their wanderings in the wilderness. Both were presumably true. The covenant relationship between Jehovah and Israel was born in the heart of the Eternal and was not dependent upon the sacrificial system. It was reflected in the devotion of the beneficiaries and maintained by the unchanging God.

It is equally clear, however, that the requirements prescribed in the law did, to a great extent, fall into desuetude—although not entirely so, for Num. 17: 46 indicates that the altar fire continued to burn, doubtless for the offering of the daily sacrifice. Jehovah may, therefore, have been referring to the idolatry of the people in that earlier period, so typical of their conduct in the later day of Amos. This is the view taken by W. Manson (*The Epistle to the Hebrews,* p. 30), where, referring to Stephen's speech in Acts 7, he writes, "what Amos meant, according to Stephen, was not that God had not commanded sacrifices and oblations, but that Israel had diverted its offering and its sanctuary to idolatrous purposes."

If this interpretation is accepted as the most logical, there was also the implication of punishment in His words: as those of Moses's day were excluded from Canaan, those of Amos's day might be excluded from blessing. As E. W. Hengstenberg says (*Dissertations on the Pentateuch,* vol. 1, p. 157), "All this (the acts of worship enumerated in vv. 21-23) can no more be called a true worship, than the open idolatry in the wilderness. Therefore, as in that instance, the outwardly idolatrous people did not tread the holy land, so now will the inwardly idolatrous people be driven out of the holy land."

THE PENALTY OF IDOLATRY

But you have carried the booth of your Moloch and Chiun, your images, the star of your god, which you made for yourselves. Therefore, I will cause you to go into exile beyond Damascus, says Jehovah, whose name is the God of hosts (5 : 26, 27).

If they failed to give Jehovah His due honour and worship, the Israelites freely paid homage to other gods. The Massoretic text of verse 26 reads, "You shall take up Sikkut your king and Kiyun your images, the star of your gods." The word *succoth* (booth) is rendered by a number of translators as Sikkut or Sakkuth, i.e. Adar, the Assyrian god of war and the chase. Chiun has been rendered Kaiwan, the Assyrian name for Saturn, who was also worshipped as a deity. The LXX and Peshitta both refer to Moloch (or Milcom), although Driver and others insist that the Massoretic "king" is more correct. Moloch, of course, was actually an object of worship. In his defence before the Sanhedrin, Stephen quoted Amos 5 : 26 as "you took up the tabernacle of Moloch, and the star of your god Remphan, figures which you made to worship. And I will carry you away beyond Babylon" (Acts 7 : 43). His quotation was from the Septuagint and the difference in rendering was irrelevant to his argument.

Whatever translation is adopted, the accusation is clear, that the people had turned to false planetary divinities, who were represented by stars. The idols of those deities they had carried away from conquered nations and made their own. The Israelites had been exposed to the idolatrous worship of the stars and of astral deities in Egypt, and a permanent impression seems to have been made upon them by their sojourn in that country.

For their idolatry Israel was to be exiled beyond Damascus, God declared. At that time "beyond Damascus" was an unknown region. It obviously referred to Assyria, which actually deported the people of Israel, although this could probably not have been anticipated at the time. The fate pronounced patently involved the horrors of war and defeat, the spoliation of goods and the maltreatment of civilians, the captivity of the able-bodied and the violation of the women. Amos's hearers would understand the implications and realise all the sufferings predicted. This was to be their well-deserved fate.

CHAPTER 8

The Third Discourse (continued)

THE greater part of the remainder of Amos's third discourse was taken up by a diatribe against the upper echelons of society in Israel. Despite all that had been said already, they were oblivious to the real state in which they were found.

AN UNDISTURBED ARISTOCRACY
Woe to those who are at ease in Zion and to those who put their trust in the mountain of Samaria, the men of mark of the first of the nations, to whom the house of Israel comes (6 : 1).

Although the prophecy had been concerned primarily with Israel, Amos now associated Zion (Jerusalem), i.e., Judah, with their counterparts in Israel, and pronounced a woe upon those who were at ease in Zion and those who similarly placed their confidence in the mountain of Samaria. Judah and Israel alike were condemned.

They were at ease and undisturbed by any political or social consideration. No neighbouring nation was apparently in a sufficiently strong position to launch an attack upon them. They rested secure. Zion was impregnable and Samaria was unassailable. Moreover, they were convinced that they were under the protection of Jehovah and that He could not conceivably fail them. His covenant was binding upon Him. They could justifiably relax in sheer optimism.

The luxury of these leaders, who were described as men of distinction, had dulled their senses to the dangers which were threatening. They had secured economic and political control of the country and everyone was compelled to resort to them. They talked glibly of Israel as the supreme nation, "the first of the nations" and deemed themselves the notables of Israel. They ignored the responsibilities attendant on rank and position. And similar conditions were to be found in Judah.

GREATER THAN OTHERS

Pass over to Calneh and see: and from thence go to Hamath the great: then go down to Gath of the Philistines. Are they better than these kingdoms? Or is their territory greater than your territory? (6 : 2).

Realising the impossibility of arousing the nobles of Judah and Israel by normal methods, Amos—understanding full well the way they were reasoning in their position of security—employed the very thoughts which were probably filling their minds and put the thoughts into words. Were any of the surrounding nations comparable with these two kingdoms?

Ironically he puts the words into their mouths. Cross over to Calneh and see, then go on to Hamath and then down to Gath. Were any of these superior to Judah and Israel? He was merely articulating their own pride and boastful spirit. Calneh (the Calno of Isa. 10 : 9) was not identical with the city of the same name in Gen. 10 : 10, but was located near Carchemish. Hamath was an important city on the Orontes River. The mention of Gath is somewhat puzzling as it had been captured by Uzziah in 760 B.C. It was located to the west of Jerusalem.

They turned east, north and west in their pride and asked whether any of these city states could be compared with Judah and Israel. Was their territory as great? The prophet threw their boastful pride at them in his words. Was not this how they thought?

THE PAMPERED RICH

O you who put far off the evil day and bring near the seat of violence, who lie upon beds of ivory and sprawl on their couches, and eat lambs from the flock and calves from the

midst of the stall, who croon to the tune of the harp and, like
David, devise for themselves musical instruments, who drink
wine in bowls and anoint themselves with the finest ointments:
but are not grieved over the ruin of Joseph (6 : 3-6).

Repeated warnings of impending doom had been given to the impenitent sinners of Israel. The prophet had detailed their transgressions and had plainly stated that Jehovah's hand of judgment was about to fall. He had used every effort to awake them to a realisation of their jeopardy, but it was all to no avail. Evidently they had listened idly to him, but had discounted his dark prognostications as gloomy pessimism. Such things could not happen to them: they were the chosen of the Lord.

Amos was aware of their reasoning and declared that they were, at least in thought, postponing the evil day. They were living for the present and refused to consider the possibility of any radical change in circumstances. They were powerful and prosperous, they imposed their policies on others and, by their corruption, ensured that there was no opposition, they ground down the poor and expropriated their heritage. Their resources and revenues were surely clear evidences of the blessing of heaven.

The prophet might talk of a day of reckoning, but they dismissed this as an idle tale. Their security was obvious: nothing could disturb their condition. If there was a judgment day to come, it had no relevance to them, and they could not conceive of anything of that character in the foreseeable future. In their minds, therefore, they superciliously postponed it indefinitely. This prophet of the south was completely out of touch with reality. So they may well have reasoned.

Yet Amos declared that their very attempts to put off the evil day were only precipitating the judgment they ridiculed. They were hastening the coming of the seat of violence. (The word "seat" was used in the technical sense of a judicial seat, as in Psa. 122 : 5.) In the misfortune they created by their constant oppression of others, they acted violently. But they were digging their own graves, for violence was to come upon them.

The Peshitta version reads "cause the sabbath of violence to come near," and this has often been connected by expositors with the violent attack of the enemy which, often in Israel's history had happened on the sabbath day, because the foe had been aware of their reluctance to take any action on the sabbath. This, however, is a little far-fetched. The plain inference is that, although they refused to accept the concept of an impending judgment and dismissed the idea to the remote future, their very conduct only brought the day of reckoning nearer.

Amos turned upon them and scathingly described their manner of life. When others would sit on rugs and carpets, they lolled upon beds inlaid with ivory, they sprawled out on their comfortable couches in indolent ease. Only the succulent food was suitable for these gourmets—tender lambs from the flock and calves from the fattening stall. No expense was too great for their entertainment: their luxurious sophistication was far in advance of their time.

It was not their wealth or their enjoyment of the material benefits of life which the prophet criticised, but rather the methods by which they had been acquired and the attitude they displayed towards them. The Bible does not demand asceticism or prohibit the enjoyment of the blessings God bestows, provided there is the true spirit of thankfulness to the One who is the donor of it all. But a practice of unreserved self-indulgence at the expense of others or in the presence of others' need is well deserving of the strictures of Amos. Yet such heedless hedonism is not entirely missing today. One part of the world starves, while another lives in affluence. For the Christian, there is no dubiety as to the manner of life to be adopted; the A.V. rendering of Phil. 4 : 5 is not without its significance.

As they reclined at their loaded tables, the blasé Israelites sought musical entertainment to lighten their day. Idle improvisation took place as they crooned to the sound of the harp. Additionally, "the same pains, which David employed on music to the honour of God, they employed on their light enervating, unmeaning music and, if they were in earnest enough, justified their inventions by the example of David" (Pusey, *ibid*, p. 308). Was this honouring to God?

The description ought not to be lightly dismissed as having no current relevance. The effects of modern music (if that is the correct term) have been the subject of so many articles and books that no comment is needed here. One writer's remarks are very pertinent, "Debased music is a mark of a nation's decay and promotes it."

Still gazing in imagination at the scene he had conjured up, Amos pictured these self-indulgent upper-class citizens fanning the passions, kindled by voluptuous music and fed by rich food, by drinking wine in bowlfuls. The word he used for "bowls" was that appropriate to those from which the blood of the sacrificial victim was sprinkled. These idle rich cared nothing for the ritual purpose: the bowl must serve their personal desire. They were not content to drink a modicum of wine to accompany their food, but must gulp down bowlfuls in drunken haste.

They anointed their bodies with the most expensive ointments, using what might more appropriately have been offered to God (cf. John 12 : 3). Anointing was commonly suspended at times of mourning (2 Sam. 14 : 2), but there was no sorrow on the part of these people and they, therefore, demanded the best unguents. Yet this was the time when they should have been mourning.

They did not grieve over the ruin of Joseph (i.e. their own country), complained the prophet. But the country was at the height of prosperity: what cause was there for grief? Their own flesh and blood were suffering because of the afflictions caused by their own oppression. The needy were turned aside in the gate. Was there not reason for tears? But these wealthy dilettantes had no tears to shed. Their comfortable circumstances excluded all thought of the suffering world outside. Their attitude was their own condemnation. They were "not grieved over the ruin of Joseph."

THE ASSYRIAN CAPTIVITY

Therefore now they shall go into exile at the head of those who go into exile, and the revelry of those who stretched themselves shall pass away. Adonai Jehovah has sworn by himself, says Jehovah the God of hosts, I abhor the pride of Jacob and hate his strongholds. Therefore I will deliver up the city with all that is in it (6 : 7, 8).

These men had sought eminence socially, commercially and politically. They had attained the status after which they had striven and indulged themselves to the full. Amos declared that, when the day of trouble came, they should still retain their priority. When the Assyrians swept away thousands into captivity, they should be the first to go. They were, in fact, in the vanguard of the 28,000 captives whom Sargon II deported. With tragic irony, the prophet depicts them leading the pitiful column out of the country.

The sounds of their revelry had been heard far and wide. They lay dissolutely stretched out on their couches, drunkenly screaming in reckless abandon. All that would end. The sounds would die away, leaving only an ominous silence. The mirth of today would be swallowed up in the misery of tomorrow. It was a vivid picture, but the recompense was just.

Three times in his book Amos stated that Jehovah had sworn. In 4 : 2 it was by His holiness; in 6 : 8 by Himself; and in 8 : 7 by the excellency or pride of Jacob. God's word is final and conclusive, but if He swears by Himself as an additional confirmation, the word is not merely binding, but of the utmost gravity. Here Amos stated that the Lord God, Adonai Jehovah, had sworn by Himself. There could be no possible doubt consequently about what was to follow. What He declared He would do must inevitably come to pass. The decision was immutable.

He first announced that He abhorred the pride of Jacob and hated its strongholds. The overwhelming conceit of those who had seized position and power in Israel convinced them that they were invulnerable against any opposition. Not only were they satisfielid regarding their security and the permanence of their state of comfort, but they boasted that what they had achieved had been by their own efforts.

Since no one can boast of possessing anything which is not, either directly or indirectly, the gift of God, the one who lifts himself up in pride and who claims to have accomplished by his own ability, is virtually denying the supremacy of God. In His presence there is no room for pride, and before Him no braggart may utter his boasts. Pride is an abomination to Him. It is perhaps significant that Israel was "called by the name of its sinful father, who selfishly sought his own advantage by fair means or foul." It was the "pride of Jacob" that God abhorred.

If they denied the lordship of Jehovah by their pride, they equally denied His character by their claim to security. They had their defences and fortifications (built at the price of their exaction from the poor) and regarded these as completely invulnerable. Yet the essence of Jehovah's relationship with Israel was that He was their shelter and their Rock. Their self-confidence was completely misplaced. If He did not protect them, their strongholds were utterly useless. He hated their pretentious claim to self-sufficiency and the basis on which it was made.

Their moral obliquity had reached its limit, and Jehovah now declared plainly that His intention was to deliver up Samaria and all it contained. Nothing now could avert the judgment which had been threatened. Their doom was certain. It was not long before the Assyrians captured Samaria and carried away captive all its inhabitants and plundered all its treasures. The prophecy was completely fulfilled.

THE PESTILENCE

Then it shall be that, if ten men remain in one house, they shall die. And a man's kinsman and he who burns him will take him up to bring the bones out of the house, and will say to him who is in the inner part of the house, Is there anyone still with you? And he will say, No. Then he will say, Hush! We must not mention the name of Jehovah (6 : 9, 10).

The siege which Amos had virtually predicted would, of course, result in the death of many of the defenders of the city. But, as was common in war, military conflict was not the only foe. The privations of the siege would probably result in the death of others by starvation or malnutrition. The prophet contemplated that, in addition, a plague—as so often happened in such circumstances—would sweep through the city and that large numbers would die as a result of the pestilence.

He drew a very vivid picture of one large house in which ten men were sheltering, and implied that the plague would strike the house and that all would die. It was necessary that the bodies should be removed to avoid contagion spreading, but the number of dead in the city were too many to permit of the normal practice of burial. The corpses were, therefore, removed to be cremated. This was not a generally accepted funeral practice in Israel, except for criminals (Lev. 20 : 14; 21 : 9), and only the exceptional circumstances would be deemed to justify it.

Accompanied by the one responsible for the cremation of bodies, the kinsman came to the house of which Amos spoke, for the purpose of removing the body of one of the men. All the occupants appeared to have died but, to make sure, he called to a survivor within, to ask if anyone else was left. Replying in the negative, the man who remained added, "Hush! We must not mention the name of Jehovah."

It has been suggested that he feared that the mention of Jehovah's name would invoke a further curse upon the house. It was He who had inflicted war, famine, pestilence and death, and the survivor feared to attract attention to himself lest he too should suffer the same fate. Others have suggested that it was in the realisation of the sin, which had caused the outpouring of judgment, that the survivor confessed that they had no claim upon Jehovah: the punishment was justified by the guilt, and there was no plea that could possibly be presented for alleviation. It is more probable, however, that it was the fear of a further infliction which was envisioned.

COMPLETE DESTRUCTION

For, behold, Jehovah commands, and he will smite the great house into fragments and the little house into splinters (6 : 11).

The destruction to come upon Samaria was to be complete. The instructions were issued by God, and He announced that rich and poor would suffer. The great, luxurious, stone-built houses of the wealthy and noble would be shattered into fragments. The cottages of the lowly would be broken into splinters or small particles. None would escape. High and low would come under His hand.

The Targum maintains that the great house is Israel and the little house Judah, but there is nothing to support this idea.

PERVERSION OF RIGHT

Do horses run upon rocks? Does one plough the sea with oxen? Yet you have turned justice into gall, and the fruit of righteousness into wormwood (6 : 12).

In the typical eastern style, Amos posed questions to his hearers to which there could be only one reply. "Do horses run upon rocks?" It would be absurd to expect horses to race along steep, inaccessible cliffs, suitable only for the wild goat.

"Does one plough the sea with oxen?" The question conjured up a ridiculous picture. Not only would one not take such an action, but it would be utterly pointless to attempt.

The answer in each case was obviously a negative one. Yet, he declared, Israel had taken a course which was utterly absurd and completely wrong and from which nothing could be gained. They had "turned justice into gall" and had converted "the fruit of righteousness into wormwood." God demanded justice between man and man, but they had made it bitterness. Their whole life was directed to personal profit and they had rejected the ways of true life. Could one live by this means? The answer was as clearly "No" as to the two questions the prophet posed. Israel's folly was evident.

EMPTY VICTORY

You who rejoice in Lodebar, who say, Have we not by our own strength taken Karnaim for ourselves? (6 : 13).

Jehovah was Israel's strength on the battlefield in earlier days, but now they prided themselves on their strength and ability. Had they achieved very great victories? They had indeed captured a couple of small cities on the east of the Jordan. Was this some tremendous military success of which to boast?

Amos taunted them with rejoicing in Lodebar, which meant literally "a thing of nought", and glorying in the fact that by their own strength they had captured Karnaim (literally "horns" or "strength"). This was a feeble basis for boasting. Their glorious victories were insignificant. Yet they had been encouraged by such minor successes as these. Because of these, they imagined themselves capable of facing every foe. How many a servant of Christ is guilty of the same folly! Given a small encouragement, his ego is inflated and he feels himself capable of great things. But all power is derived from God and in Him alone is spiritual success. This was the lesson Israel failed to learn.

Mays (*ibid*, p. 122) says, "The background of Israel's self-congratulation lay in the remarkable resurgence of national power which Israel had experienced under Jeroboam II. With his constant adversary, Damascus, crippled by Assyrian campaigning, Jeroboam had been able to recoup Israel's previous losses east of the Jordan; 2 Kings 14 : 25 implies that Jeroboam had recovered all the territory in that quarter which Israel had ever held." This may have been a reason for praising God, but certainly not for self-congratulation, and the victory to which the prophet referred was scarcely one for public celebrations.

THE ASSYRIAN THREAT

For, behold, I will raise up against you a nation, O house of Israel, says Jehovah, the God of hosts; and they shall oppress you from the entrance of Hamath to the brook of the Arabah (6 : 14).

While Israel rejoiced over minor successes, Jehovah declared that He was raising up a nation against them, who would oppress them from the entrance of Hamath (the pass between the Lebanons) to the brook of Arabah (either the river Arnon near the north border of Moab, or the brook Zared at the south end of the Dead Sea). The area covered would be from the northern extremity of Israel to the southern extremity: in other words, the whole country. No part of the kingdom would be spared. They would be harried and harassed from north to south.

They had boasted of their accomplishments by their own strength. Jehovah would now show His power by the instrument He would employ for their castigation. He did not disclose that it was the Assyrians that He intended to use. "In the existing state of things," wrote Keil (*ibid*, p. 235), "the idea of the approaching fall or destruction of the kindom of Israel was, according to human judgment, a very improbable one indeed. The inhabitants of Samaria and Zion felt themselves perfectly secure in the consciousness of their might (ch. 6 : 1). The rulers of the kingdom trusted in the strength of their military resources (ch. 6 : 13)."

CHAPTER 9

Priest and Prophet

AMOS was from the country of Judah and the question may well have arisen in the minds of his hearers why God should allegedly have sent a prophet from the south to speak to them rather than using one of their own fellow-countrymen. How could this man prove his credentials or authenticate his messages? It was to answer this unuttered doubt that four visions were given to the prophet. The visions were all cast in the same form. The same introductory formula in each case stated that Adonai Jehovah had shown the vision to him. The details of the vision were preceded by the cry to behold. There then followed a dialogue between the prophet and Jehovah, concluding in the first two cases with an appeal by Amos that the people might be spared. The series of visions was interrupted in 7 : 10-17 by the incident of Amaziah's opposition. While they were, to some extent, polemical, in that they were a defence of the prophet's message and authority, they had a direct minatory message to Israel as well. It is probably unnecessary to point out that *prima facie*, the visions could not have all been given on the same day, as is often concluded, since the first relates to the spring and the last to the autumn.

THE LOCUSTS

Thus Adonai Jehovah showed me: behold, he was forming locusts in the beginning of the shooting up of the latter growth; and, lo, it was the latter growth after the king's mow-

ings. When they had finished eating the grass of the land, I said, O Adonai Jehovah, forgive, I beseech thee. How can Jacob stand? He is so small. Jehovah repented concerning this. It shall not happen, says Jehovah (7 : 1-3).

The first vision was of a swarm of locusts being prepared by Jehovah for their work of devastation. The time was set as "the beginning of the shooting up of the latter growth." This clearly related to the rapid growth of the crops after the rains in March and April. It was further stated that it was "the latter growth after the king's mowings." This appears to be the only Biblical reference to the king's mowings. It is known that the Roman governors of Syria levied a tax on pasture land in the month Nisan to obtain food for their horses, and it is probable that a similar practice was followed by the rulers of Israel. Once this had been paid, the people would naturally anticipate the later growth to meet the needs of their own cattle and flocks.

Keil again takes a symbolic view of the facts. He says (*ibid*, p. 307), "The king who has had the early grass mown is Jehovah; and the mowing of the grass denotes the judgments which Jehovah had already executed upon Israel. The growing of the second crop is a figurative representation of the prosperity which flourished again after those judgments; in actual fact, it denotes the times when the dawn had risen again for Israel." It seems more reasonable, however, to take the story in a more literal sense.

Just at the critical time, the swarm of locusts swept ravenously over the land and devoured every green thing—not only grass but herbs and vegetables as well. Locusts were one of the greatest scourges of the day. When they had eaten their way across the land, nothing was left, and the despairing inhabitants were confronted with imminent famine. It was a menace against which they were helpless. Since the locust was regarded as the instrument of God's curse (Deut. 28 : 38), the people's despondency was all the greater. The hand of Jehovah was against them.

Just at that crucial juncture, when there seemed no possibility of survival, Amos assumed the role of intercessor and prayed God to forgive His people. If He declined to do so, how could they stand? Jehovah was their only real support and protection. They prided themselves upon their invulnerability to trouble, upon their security and their strength. But Amos confessed that they were only small. (It is significant that he employs the name Jacob for Israel—the reminder of the shifty character of their ancestor.) If this stroke was not lifted, it would be too much to bear.

Jehovah, in His mercy, listened to His servant's cry and announced that complete destruction should not happen. Verse 3 states that Jehovah repented concerning the matter. This did not, of course, imply a regret for action taken or proposed. As R. L. Smith (*Amos,* p. 125) writes, "Repent, when it is used of God, does not include any sense of sin, error or wrongdoing on the part of God. It does suggest perhaps a sense of sorrow that judgment has been necessary. It is an anthropopathism frequently used by the Scripture writers."

It is interesting to note that Amos fulfilled the time-honoured role of the prophet. He was not merely the spokesman of God to the people, but an intercessor on behalf of the people with God. His predecessors in the prophetic line had set the precedent long before (e.g. 1 Sam. 7 : 8).

THE FIRE

Thus Adonai Jehovah showed me: behold, Adonai Jehovah was calling for judgment by fire, and it consumed the great deep and was eating up the land. Then I said, O Adonai Jehovah, cease, I beseech thee. How can Jacob stand? He is so small. Jehovah repented concerning this. This also shall not happen, says Adonai Jehovah (7 : 4-6).

In the second vision the prophet was shown Jehovah calling for judgment by fire. He saw the great conflagration break out and sweep across the countryside, licking up the water and devastating the land of Israel. After the infliction of the locust hordes, the land would have been quite dry and, scorched by the sun, would be only too readily set ablaze by the hot rays.

The "great deep" was the term given to the subterranean waters (Gen. 7 : 11). In our twentieth century we are more aware of the existence of such waters than the Hebrews possibly were. If these were evaporated by the heat of the flame, there could be serious consequences for the earth's crust in the immediate locality, and the prophet described the effect as "eating up the apportioned land," i.e. the territory allocated to Israel.

Fire is consistently used in the Bible as a symbol of the wrath of God, culminating, of course, in the fate of the impenitent in the lake of fire (Rev. 20 : 15). If the consuming wrath of God swept over His people without mitigation, the result would be utter destruction.

Hence the prophet again intervened on behalf of Israel. In the first vision he besought Jehovah to forgive them, but in the second he merely begged Him to stop the course of the flame, using the same plea that Jacob was so small and, therefore, unable to bear the infliction. Once again, it is recorded that Jehovah repented and declared that it should not happen.

There is probably more than a hint in the vision of the judgment by the Assyrian invasion, the full effect of which, from the human point of view, was inexplicably postponed. Indeed, Pusey (*ibid*, pp. 317-8) asks, "To human sight, what so strange and unexpected as that the Assyrian and his army, having utterly destroyed the kingdom of Damascus and carried away its people, and having devoured, like fire, more than half of Israel, rolled back like an ebb tide, swept away to ravage other countries, and spared the capital? And who, looking at the mere outside of things, would have thought that that tide of fire was rolled back, not by anything in that day, but by the prophet's prayer some 47 years before? Man would look doubtless for motives of human policy, which led Tiglath-Pileser to accept tribute from Pekah, while he killed Rezin; and while he carried off all the Syrians of Damascus, to leave half of Israel to be removed by his successor.

Humanly speaking, it was a mistake. He 'scotched' his enemy only and left him to make alliance with Egypt, his rival, who disputed with him the possession of the countries which lay between them."

THE PLUMBLINE

Thus he showed me: behold, Adonai was standing beside a wall built with a plumbline, with a plumbline in his hand. And Jehovah said to me, Amos, what do you see? And I said, A plumbline. Then said Adonai, Behold, I am setting a plumbline in the midst of my people Israel. I will never again pass by them. And the high places of Isaac shall be made desolate, and the sanctuaries of Israel shall be laid waste; and I will rise up against the house of Jeroboam with the sword (7 : 7-9).

Amos saw the heavenly Sovereign standing by a wall, which had once stood perfectly perpendicular, built aright by the use of the plumbline. But now the plumbline was applied to a wall which was apparently beginning to crack and bow and to evidence signs of deviation from the perpendicular. The wall was clearly a symbol of Israel, for God declared that He was setting a plumbline in the midst of His people. He had made them, He had provided the standard for their conduct, but the wall was no longer safe and must be levelled to the ground. Israel had deviated from the rule of conduct to such an extent that there was no alternative. Their value had gone: their testimony for God was worthless and brought dishonour on His name.

As He held the plumbline to their lives and demonstrated their moral, social and spiritual crookedness, there was no doubt as to the action He must take. He had revoked the judgments which were about to fall on two previous occasions, in answer to the prophet's prayer. He called the prophet by name and now inferentially associated him with Himself in the decision taken. Amos presented no further plea and made no further intercession. It was evident that judgment was inevitable. The wall must be broken down.

In the past, Jehovah had passed over His people. His eye rested upon the blood that sheltered them. There was no shelter now. Never again would He pass over them. His measure was in their midst. The swinging cord with its heavy weight showed the extent of their divergence. Their fate was inescapable.

Using the name of their ancestor Isaac (see also v. 16), Jehovah declared that the high places of Isaac would be made desolate and that the sanctuaries of Israel would be utterly destroyed. The high place was so named because it was an altar or sacred site on the top of a hill in the open country. The sanctuary was an official religious centre such as those at Bethel and Dan, with its altar, temple and priesthood. The sacred sites had been allowed to continue with their schismatic rites and ceremonies, but now the day of reckoning had come and they were to be swept away. They were a mockery of the true and a deliberate deviation from the revealed purpose of God. It was Jeroboam I who had introduced Israel's imitation of Jerusalem's worship. Upon his house the sword was to fall. Jeroboam II was the representative of God upon the throne. Not only had he tolerated the false system of worship, but had permitted policies and practices to flourish which were oppressive and unjust. The ultimate responsibility was his. His dynasty was to be destroyed: his monarchy was to come to an end. The Ruler in the heavens took account of what happened on earth, and the day of reckoning drew near.

PRIEST AND KING

Then Amaziah, the priest of Bethel, sent to Jeroboam, king of Israel, saying, Amos has conspired against you in the midst of the house of Israel: the land is not able to bear all his words. For thus has Amos said, Jeroboam shall die with the sword, and Israel shall surely be led away captive out of their own land (7 : 10, 11).

The prophet's words had obviously resounded through Israel. The Scriptural record is probably a summary of his preaching and not the complete account of the contents of his messages, but the gist is perfectly clear. His condemnation of the people and their practices and his predictions regarding the forthcoming judgment were beyond misunderstanding. In some quarters, what he said was evidently regarded as seditious. In other instances, the warnings of prophets had caused internal revolts or had inspired dissidents to rebel. It may well have been assumed that the preaching of the herdman of Tekoa was a stratagem to cause the overthrow of the monarch and the ruling party. It may even have been thought that he was a paid emissary of Judah, bent on stirring up trouble and possibly inciting the people to return to their loyalty to the throne of David at Jerusalem.

Amaziah, the priest of the sanctuary at Bethel, plainly saw nothing spiritual about the prophet's messages. He did not recognise the voice of God in them, but interpreted them as merely the arguments of a political agitator. In his view, Amos was guilty of treason against the king, since he had predicted the sovereign's death, and was the potential cause of disquiet in the country because of his prophecies of judgment and exile.

He owed his position to the king, since the priesthood in Israel was appointed by the throne, and the sycophant lost no time in sending a messenger to king Jeroboam 25 miles away, warning him of the danger of allowing this prophet of Judah to wander round the country, proclaiming his message of doom. His message was not quite accurate, for he declared that Amos was conspiring against the king quite publicly among the people and that the country could not tolerate his preaching indefinitely, that he had said plainly that Jeroboam would be killed in war and that Israel would be carried captive into exile.

Amos, had not, of course, spoken treasonably, nor had he entered into any conspiracy or formed any opposition party. He was not guilty in any way of causing disaffection, and his ministry had been concerned entirely with the spiritual condition of the nation and the blatant transgressions of the people, and the inevitable consequences of their actions. Amaziah made no mention of the prophet's summons to repent, since this would plainly have resulted in a reaction against Bethel and his own sacerdotal position.

So far as the Scriptural record is concerned, there was no reaction from the king, who was possibly better informed on the subject than the priest. In any case, Jeroboam apparently took no action on the information sent to him. Consequently, the frustrated priest took the matter into his own hands.

AMAZIAH'S OPPOSITION

And Amaziah said to Amos, O seer, go, flee away to the land of Judah and eat bread there and prophesy there. But never prophesy again at Bethel, for it is the royal sanctuary, a temple of the kingdom (7 : 12, 13).

Amaziah was clearly not concerned with the substance or otherwise of Amos's preaching. He was only concerned to rid the country of one whom he regarded as a disturber of the peace and who was a threat to his own security. Whether the prophet's messages were true or not seemed completely irrelevant. "O seer," he said, "flee away to Judah and eat bread there and prophesy there."

Why should a southerner bring his prophetic messages to the northern kingdom? Let him return to his own country and pour out his predictions there. Contemptuously he bade him earn his living by prophesying in Judah, implying that Amos preached for financial return and not altruistically and under the direction of God (cf. 1 Sam. 9 : 7, 8). As a genuine servant of Jehovah, Amos was above financial considerations and was clearly not affected by the implicit threats of the priest.

Never prophesy again at Bethel, Amaziah commanded him. Bethel was a royal sanctuary and a temple of the kingdom. The temple at Jerusalem was a sanctuary of Jehovah and received its authority from Him. That at Bethel received its sanction from the king. It had been Jeroboam I who had consecrated it and who had appointed the priesthood and determined the ritual. Unconsciously Amaziah made the difference plain by his very description.

AMOS'S CALL

Then Amos answered Amaziah, I am no prophet, nor am I the son of a prophet; but I am a herdman and a dresser of sycomore trees. And Jehovah took me from following the flock, and Jehovah said to me, Go, prophesy to my people Israel (7 : 14, 15).

Amaziah had assessed Amos as a professional prophet, but Amos at once repudiated the insinuation. He was no member of the prophetic guild or school of prophets (1 Kings 20 : 35; 2 Kings 2 : 5). He was not a prophet nor the son of a prophet. He was a herdman, or a keeper of flocks, and a sycomore dresser. The sycomore was a type of fig tree, which needed hand pollination, although it has been suggested that the fruit was punctured to allow insects to escape.

Jehovah took him from following the flock and bade him to go and prophesy to His people, Israel. Without training or the normal qualifications for his task, Amos had heard the voice of the Eternal and, without hesitation, he turned from his ordinary avocation to respond to the Divine call. He had no option but to go. Jehovah had sent him. His message, therefore, was of Divine authority and anyone resisting it was resisting God.

If the Almighty calls, there is no need for fear or trepidation. The One who calls is the One who equips and empowers.. If the Divine message is sent by one of God's servants, the people must listen and obey, whatever they may think of the messenger.

AMAZIAH'S FATE

Now, therefore, hear the word of Jehovah. You say, Do not prophesy against Israel and do not preach against the house of Isaac. Therefore thus says Jehovah, Your wife shall be a prostitute in the city, and your sons and daughters shall fall by the sword, and your land shall be parcelled out by line, and you shall die in an unclean land and Israel shall surely go into exile away from its land (7 : 16, 17).

Fearing the loss of his lucrative appointment and his position of authority, Amaziah issued his order to Amos but, in doing so, he was in direct rebellion against Jehovah. The prophet had presented his credentials and had repeated the Divine message to him, but the priest obstinately refused to accept message or messenger. He was following in the company of those who had always rejected and persecuted the prophets (Acts 7 : 52). There could be only one outcome.

In stark contrast, Amos set Amaziah against Jehovah. "You say" and "Jehovah says". He repeated the priest's injunction to him not to prophesy against Israel or to preach against the house of Isaac. This was a denial of the right of God to address His people. If that was his firm attitude, then Jehovah would deal with him.

The sentence passed was fearful, although the punishment was only typical of that to be suffered by the whole nation of Israel. Judgment, which Amos had consistently threatened, would undoubtedly be executed. In that day, Amaziah's wife, no doubt proud and stately, would be exposed to public indignity. The soldiers of the invader would treat her shamelessly as a prostitute (Isa. 13 : 16; Zech. 14 : 2) to be used and abused at will—and this in the city where her shame could not be hidden. His sons and daughters would be killed in the conflict. His property would be parcelled out by lot among the victors (2 Kings 17 : 24). He, who scrupulously preserved himself from defilement because of his office, would be carried away to die in an unknown land (i.e. a land which was devoted to the worship of false gods and was, therefore, ceremonially unclean to a priest of Jehovah). Once again also Amos declared that the people of Israel would be deported from their own land (as, of course, actually occurred at the Assyrian conquest).

In attempting to silence Amos, Amaziah had endeavoured to silence God. For that he was divested of office and everything he valued was taken from him. It is a serious thing to challenge the Almighty.

CHAPTER 10

The Corrupt Nation

WE ARE not told whether Amos returned to Judah after the interposition of Amaziah, but it seems unlikely. It is more probable that the remaining messages of the book were delivered in the northern kingdom to which he had been sent. The incident with the priest appeared as a parenthesis between the third and fourth of the prophet's visions. Having pronounced the priest's sentence, Amos reverted to the visions once more.

THE SUMMER FRUIT

Thus Adonai Jehovah showed me: behold a basket of summer fruit. And he said, Amos, what do you see? And I said, A basket of summer fruit. Then said Jehovah to me, The end has come upon my people of Israel. I will never again pass by them. The songs of the palace will become wailings in that day, says Adonai Jehovah. Many will be the corpses cast out everywhere. Hush! (8 : 1-3).

The fourth vision given to the prophet was of a basket of summer fruit. It has been concluded by some expositors that this represented an offering brought to Bethel by a worshipper at the time of the autumn festival, but the point is immaterial. The gathering of the summer fruit occurred at the end of the harvest, and the vision, therefore, implied that the harvest was completed (Matt. 13 : 39).

The significance of the vision was explained by Jehovah. Just as the contents of the basket indicated the end of the harvest, so the end had come for His people Israel. Their harvest was now to come, for they were ripe for judgment. No longer could their sin be passed over. Laetsch (*ibid*, p. 180) points out that "the Lord turns the term 'summer fruit' (*kayits*), used by the prophet, into a very effective play on words, 'The end (*qets*) is come upon my people Israel'." It was too late now for penitence. The end had come.

"I will never again pass by them," said the heavenly voice. Never again would mercy cover their transgressions or compassion enfold them. God would not pass them by. Judgment now was imminent. "In that day"—a term used of the day of Jehovah, the awful period of judgment—joy would give place to sorrow. The harvest time was one of feasting and happiness, but the songs which filled the palace (or possibly the temple) would then be transformed into the wailing lamentations of mourners. The dead would be so numerous that burial would be impossible. The bodies would be thrown out everywhere: the ordinary funeral rites would be denied them and the bereaved in their tragic sorrow would cry, "Hush!" This was not merely the exclamation of grief, but an acknowledgment that nothing could be said in the presence of the One who inflicted the blow.

THE DISHONEST TRADERS

Hear this, you who trample upon the needy and cause the poor of the land to cease, saying, When will the new moon be gone, that we may sell grain? And the sabbath that we may offer wheat for sale, that we may make the ephah small and the shekel large, and deal deceitfully with false balances? That we may buy the poor for silver and the needy for a pair of sandals, and sell the refuse of the wheat? (8 : 4-6).

The prophet then turned to the traders who had exploited the poor and called upon them to listen to his indictment. He declared that they had trampled upon the needy and were bringing the poor of the land to their end. Human misery meant nothing to these callous merchants. They were prepared to crush the unfortunate to extract the last ounce from them.

By their consistent oppression they were forcing the poor to the limit of their endurance. Yet they recked not what happened: if the impoverished perished, it provided the opportunity to seize his land and add it to their own. They were utterly unscrupulous in their determination to seize every material benefit they could.

Their religious observances were a sheer mockery. They could scarcely wait for the religious activities to conclude so that they could proceed with their ruthless prosecution of their own interests. "When will the new moon be gone that we may sell grain?" they asked. "And the sabbath that we may offer wheat for sale?" Holy days meant nothing to them: they were simply a hindrance to their occupation with what mattered far more to them. Once the holy days were over, they could get on with their business.

They are not without their counterparts today, of course—those who regard time spent on religious activities as a nuisance and an appalling waste of time which might be better occupied in the pursuit of normal business.

Amos tore the rags of hypocrisy off them and exposed their true character. He accused them of making the ephah small and the shekel large and dealing deceitfully with false balances. The ephah was a unit of dry measure which the vendor used to weigh out the grain for the purchaser. The normal capacity was just over a bushel, but these dishonest merchants made the container smaller than it should have been, so that the purchasers were consistently defrauded.

The shekel was the basic unit of weight (about half an ounce) and the amount paid by the purchaser was weighed against the seller's shekel. In an attempt to secure further usurious gains, the merchants deliberately increased the weight of the shekel used as a weight. The unfortunate purchaser consequently paid more and received less. A specimen of these weighted shekels is in the Ashmolean Museum at Oxford: it represents 156 grains instead of 135. At Tirzah two sets of weights were found, one for buying and the other for selling. The deceit was carried even farther, for false balances were also used, a practice strictly prohibited (Lev. 19: 35-37; Deut. 25 : 13-15). To make matters even worse, profits were increased still more by selling the refuse (i.e. the chaff and trash left after winnowing) as good wheat.

The original practice of farmers selling their own produce direct had given way to a commercial system in which the merchants monopolised the market, stockpiling grain, etc., and virtually controlling the economy. They could, therefore, charge exorbitant prices and the purchasers had no remedy. Their avarice drove many of the poorer into a state of penury. In some cases, the latter were reduced to such straits that they had no alternative but to sell themselves for a paltry piece of silver or even for a pair of sandals, so abject was their poverty. Eventually, therefore, their relentless oppressors not only defrauded them of all their possessions, but bought them at a low price as slaves. Their conditions were deplorable to the extreme, and it is little wonder that the wrath of God fell upon them.

THE EARTHQUAKE

Jehovah has sworn by the pride of Jacob, I will never forget any of their deeds. Shall not, on this account, the earth tremble and everyone who lives in it mourn? All of it shall rise up like the Nile; and it shall be tossed about and sink again like the Nile of Egypt And on that day, says Adonai Jehovah, I will cause the sun to set at noon and I will darken the earth in broad daylight (8 : 7-9).

The conduct of the merchants and traders was so intolerable that condign punishment was inevitable. Jehovah bound Himself by oath never to forget any of their deeds. They must inescapably be called to account for them. He swore by the pride or excellency of Jacob, i.e. by Himself.

The judgment He announced was that which was the constant fear—an earthquake. It was specifically linked with their disgraceful behaviour: it was "on this account" that the land was subjected to this physical disturbance. When the earth trembled, the inhabitants would naturally lament: security had gone and their lives and possessions were threatened and there was no escape.

The upheavals and convulsions of the earth were pictured as the rising and sinking of the Nile at the time of the annual inundation. It was a fit symbol of the earthquake (cf. Isa. 24 : 19, 20). The disaster would be no mere natural happening: it was the hand of God at work to punish the guilty inhabitants of Israel. Nothing could avert their suffering, which was only the due retribution for their deeds.

The earthquake would be accompanied, the prophet declared, by an eclipse of the sun. To the onlooker, it would appear that the sun had set at noonday, and the broad daylight would suddenly be blotted out and the land plunged into darkness. There was, in fact, a total eclipse of the sun in Israel on June 15th, 763 B.C., and the reference may possibly be to that occurrence.

Any happening to the celestial bodies was always regarded as a catastrophe. Treating it allegorically, Keil (*ibid*, p. 317) writes, "to any man the sun sets at noon when he is suddenly snatched away by death, in the very midst of his life. And this also applies to a nation when it is suddenly destroyed in the midst of earthly prosperity. But it has a still wider application when the Lord shall come to judgment, at a time when the world, in its self-security, looks not for him (cf. Matt. 24 : 37 sqq.), this earth's sun will set at noon, and the earth be covered with darkness in bright daylight." While the description given may have an application to the judgment which still lies in the future, the primary interpretation must be a literal one to the people of Israel at that time.

JOY INTO TRAGEDY
I will turn your feasts into mourning, and all your songs into a dirge; and I will put sackcloth upon all loins and baldness on every head; and I will make it like the mourning for an only son and its end like a bitter day (8 : 10).

There was to be no amelioration of the suffering and anguish caused by the punitive hand of the Almighty. The festivals of Israel were times of happiness and rejoicing, however insincere the sentiments expressed may have been; but sorrow was to sweep over the people, and mourning would take the place of joy. In the realisation of the extent of the calamity and possibly an awareness that it was due to the judgment of God, the people could only give themselves over to grief. Their songs of exultation at the festivals would be transformed into a dirge associated with a funeral. The implication, moreover, was that it should be a continuous wailing and not merely restricted to a limited period. There was reason for the grief.

At a time of personal grief or bereavement or at a time of national calamity, it was the custom to wear a sackcloth garment round the loins (2 Sam. 3 : 31) and also to shave the head as a further sign of mourning, despite the fact that this was forbidden by the law (Deut. 14 : 1). The mourning was to be comparable to the sorrow experienced at the loss of an only son. Only sons could carry on the family name: the loss of an only son was a heavy blow, but this was the type of grief which would come upon these fraudulent and oppressive Israelites. Well might the prophet describe its end as like a bitter day. Yet they could scarcely complain that it was not well-deserved.

Nothing escapes the eye of God. He may allow men to continue unchecked for a long time. He may seem to wink at their sin. But the day of reckoning must come sooner or later. His perfect justice and equity compel Him to act eventually.

SPIRITUAL FAMINE

Behold the days are coming, says Adonai Jehovah, when I will send a famine in the land; not a famine of bread nor a thirst for water, but of hearing the words of Jehovah. They shall totter from sea to sea, and from north to east. They shall run to and fro to seek the word of Jehovah, but shall not find it. In that day shall the fair maids and young men faint for thirst (8 : 11-13).

The judgment which was to fall upon Israel was of a character unparalleled in their history. In announcing it, Jehovah used an eschatological formula as an introduction, "the days are coming." What was described may have had a partial fulfilment in the days of Amos, but the complete fulfilment is yet to be seen.

He declared that He would send an unusual famine in the land. The normal association of a famine was with a drought. In consequence of the latter, the grass and crops were withered and there was no food, the rivers and brooks dried up and there was no water. People hungered for bread and thirsted for water, but there was no satisfaction of their basic needs for the sustenance of life.

What was now predicted, however, was not physical but spiritual disaster. God was about to impose a famine "of hearing the words of Jehovah." The people had had the opportunity of listening to the oracles of the prophets and had disregarded them. Amos had come to them with the warnings of Jehovah and they had refused to listen. Now the voice of the prophets would die away and there would be no revelation from heaven. This was, of course, fulfilled at the close of the prophetic ministry of Malachi. For four centuries no voice broke the silence with a direct message from God, until the final revelation came in the Person of His Son. It may be that there is also a reference to a day still future.

When men were in trouble, they betook themselves to a prophet or seer for guidance or enlightenment, and usually received direction regarding the course to follow or the decision to be made. In times of national crisis, the kingdom turned to the sanctuaries where God was worshipped and sought a response from Jehovah to their current need. All that was finished. God had decided to turn away from them and abandon them to their fate (Psa. 74 : 9). If there was no Divine communication, the implication was that God had either disowned His people or was not prepared to intervene on their behalf.

With a sudden realisation of their loss, the people would send to every part of the land in a search for some contact with God, something to satisfy their spiritual hunger and to assuage their spiritual thirst; but there was nothing. Amos pictured them as running to and fro and feebly tottering from sea to sea and from north to east. Bewildered and perplexed, they would make a complete circuit of the country in fruitless endeavour. From the Dead Sea to the Mediterranean, and from Dan to Beersheba, they would search, and run to and fro across the country, but it was all to no avail.

Even the young men and women, with all their physical vigour and vitality, would swoon from exhaustion, or faint from thirst. On every side there would be the longing to find some response from Jehovah, but there was no hope. The heavens would be as brass to their cries.

The warning of over two and a half millennia ago is not without its pertinence to the present day. Countries, which once knew and honoured God and His Word, turned their backs upon Him and refused to listen to His Word. The Scriptures have been ridiculed and despised and every effort made (even by men masquerading as Christian leaders) to discredit them. The One who sits upon the throne is not ignorant of the waywardness of man and it may be that, in our time also, the Holy Spirit will cease to strive with man and that the Word of God may no longer speak to those who despise it. It was a serious warning in Amos's day.

IDOLATROUS WORSHIPPERS

Those who swear by the guilt of Samaria and say, As your god lives, O Dan, and as the way of Beersheba lives, they shall fall and never rise again (8 : 14).

The sentence upon those, who worshipped Jehovah in an idolatrous fashion or in a different manner than He had ordained, was then pronounced. They were described as "Those who swear by the guilt of Samaria." It is usually thought that, by "the guilt of Samaria", the prophet intended the golden calf at Bethel and that at Dan (Deut. 9 : 21 refers to the golden calf as Israel's sin). It has, however, been suggested that he referred to the goddess Ashimah, who was worshipped at Hamath (2 Kings 17 : 30) and possibly elsewhere. The Elephantine papyri of Egypt of a couple of centuries later designate her as Asham-Bethel and it is known that she was worshipped by the Jewish colony at Elephantine. On the other hand, the reference may have been to the Canaanite goddess, Ashera. The sentence of Jehovah upon these was related to the fact that their oaths were by the deity of Samaria and, therefore, a direct insult to Himself.

Again they made their affirmation by the deity of Dan—"As your god lives, O Dan." There were probably those who swore by the golden calf at Dan or possibly others who addressed Jehovah by an appellation used in Dan, but both were clearly disapproved.

Others swore by "the way of Beersheba," the centre to which pilgrimages were so often made: as long as that way "lived", or continued to exist, it might provide a basis for an oath. It has been thought, however, that the word "way" probably concealed the name of a deity associated with Beersheba: this is not known.

Jehovah could tolerate no recognition of other gods or of the description of Himself by the names of heathen deities. Those who had followed this course would pay for their folly. They would fall and never rise again. They had virtually despised the Almighty and no hope was held out for them.

CHAPTER II

The Ultimate Blessing

THE last chapter of the Book of Amos is an extremely clear statement of the forthcoming dispersion of Israel. Centuries before, God had explicitly stated that continuance in disobedience would result in a worldwide dispersion (Deut. 28 : 63-68). This was now to be put into effect.

THE SANCTUARY SUFFERS

I saw Adonai standing beside the altar: and he said, Smite the capitals that the thresholds may shake, and shatter them on the heads of all the people. And I will slay the last of them with the sword. Not a fugitive of them shall flee away and not a survivor of them shall escape (9 : 1).

God had declared that a spiritual famine would be the lot of His people and that there would be no message from Him, whatever the search made for it. Amos now saw Him standing beside the altar prepared to execute judgment. "The position of the Lord (Adonai) is significant," says Scofield. "The altar speaks properly of mercy because of judgment executed upon an interposed sacrifice, but when altar and sacrifice are despised the altar becomes a place of judgment." Since Amos had just denounced the idolatry of the country, the altar mentioned was presumably that of Bethel and the judgment was upon the idolatrous worship and the schismatic altar. The fact that God stood there was clear evidence of the superiority of His power to that of the false deities followed by the people.

It is significant that God was not described as Jehovah, the

God of the covenant, but as Adonai, the Sovereign. Israel had done despite to Him and despite the covenant relationship—or perhaps because of it—she must suffer. McFadyen (*in loc.*) says, "It is a vision of truly titanic power. In the temple, whose courts were crowded with infatuated worshippers, Amos saw the Lord standing beside the altar—ominous sight: for the people who there, of all places, must have felt most secure, had denied Him the service for which He supremely cared—the service of an honourable public and private life, gentle and just in all its relations; and beside the altar, reeking with their foolish sacrifices, stands the mighty God, whom they have insulted, ready to destroy them. Suddenly across the crowded courts rings out the dreadful word, Smite, addressed by the Lord to some unseen angelic minister of vengeance."

"Smite the capitals that the thresholds may shake, and shatter them on the heads of all the people," came the Divine command. Those, who identify the altar with that at Jerusalem, claim that what was described were the ornamental capitals of the two huge pillars erected in the temple by Solomon (1 Kings 7 : 21). But it is probably more appropriate to interpret it as applying to the capitals of the columns supporting the temple roof at Bethel. When these were smashed, the roof itself would collapse, and the whole would fall upon the heads of the assembled worshippers and bury them beneath the ruins (cf. Jud. 16 : 29, 30).

The people had boasted that God was with them (Am. 5: 14), but He now destroyed their sanctuary and demonstrated that there was no intercourse with Him.

The very thresholds of the building trembled as the pillars, capitals and roof fell. The "threshold" was the great stone slab on which the door posts were fixed (Isa. 6 : 4). The blow fell from above and the whole building was shaken to its foundations, "In the temple . . . the idolatrous nation beheld an indestructible pledge of the lasting continuance of the kingdom. But this support to their false trust is taken away from them by the announcement that the Lord will lay the temple to ruins." Perhaps now they realised that God had deserted them and that they had taken His name in vain.

Crowds would have been crushed to death in the fall of the temple, but no one was to be allowed to escape. Those who remained would perish subsequently by the sword. No fugitive would be permitted to flee and not a survivor would escape. It was to be the most calamitous period in Israel's history. The God, whose worshippers they claimed to be, had shown His rejection of them in this total destruction.

NO ESCAPE

Though they dig through to Sheol, from thence will my hand take them. Though they climb up to heaven, from thence will I bring them down. Though they hide themselves on the top of Carmel, I will search out and take them from thence. Though they hide themselves from my sight at the bottom of the sea, there will I command the serpent and it will bite them. Though they go into exile before their enemies, there will I command the sword and it will slay them: and I will set my eyes upon them for evil and not for good (9 : 2-4).

No one would escape the determined holocaust. God's anger would be poured out inexorably and determinedly. The people might seek refuge in the heights above or the depths beneath, but no hiding place could conceal them from the omniscient and omnipotent One. "Sheol and heaven mark off cosmic limits," says one writer, "the top of Carmel and the bottom of the sea the extremes of height and depth on earth," but no place was outside the reach of the Almighty (Psa. 139 : 7-12).

If it was possible for mortal man to reach the inaccessible depths of Sheol or the transcendent heights of heaven, he would not be beyond the hand of the Eternal. What hope was there of escape? Carmel abounded in caves and, at that time, its summit was thickly wooded: Strabo said in the 1st century A.D. that its impenetrable forests were the secret haunt of robbers. Yet Carmel would provide no shelter for Israel's sinners when God sought them out. If it was possible to seek a refuge on the bed of the ocean, it would prove inadequate, for God declared that He could direct the sea-serpent (the venomous and ferocious hydrophidae) to attack the fugitive. The position was hopeless: there was no hiding-place from His eyes.

They had already been threatened with exile, but now the Almighty indicated that this would provide no protection for them. The shame of captivity and the humiliation and degradation to which they would be subjected were sufficient in themselves, but this was not the climax. They would not be safe in exile, for He would command the sword to slay them. Destruction would follow them even into Assyria.

There was no hope, "I will set My eyes upon them for evil and not for good," came the Divine statement. Normally, the expression "set My eyes upon" implied a favourable oversight, a watching over for purposes of blessing (Jer. 24 : 6). It was now employed, not in the usual benevolent sense, but to indicate God's deliberate intention to bring trouble upon His people. They were to pay dearly for their stubborn folly and selfish ways.

THE MIGHTY GOD

Adonai Jehovah Sabaoth, he who touches the earth and it melts, and all who live in it mourn, and all of it rises like the Nile and sinks again like the Nile of Egypt; who builds his upper chambers in the heavens and founds his arch over the earth; who calls the waters of the sea and pours them out over the face of the earth: Jehovah is his name (9 : 5, 6).

Jehovah then disclosed something of His might and power, possibly as convincing evidence of His ability to perform what He had threatened to do to Israel. In poetical language, Amos declared that, when He touches the earth, it melts and rises and sinks like a river, heaving like a flood, and the terrified inhabitants give voice to their terror in mourning. The melting rocks pouring out their burning lava, the heaving land, disturbed by the earthquake, looking more like a turbulent river, all tell of the natural calamities which may be caused by the touch of the Divine finger. This was the One with whom Israel had to do.

The prophet declared that He built His upper chambers or stories in the heavens—perhaps more accurately the stairs by which was the ascent to the throne. The different heavens were sometimes referred to as the stairs to the heaven of heavens.

The vast firmament, which seems to be a massive arch over the earth, was regarded by the ancients as a solid vault, its extremities resting upon the earth. That tremendous arch, acording to Amos, was constructed by Him over the earth. (He does not imply that it rests upon the earth or that it is solid.)

The ancients again imagined that there were great reservoirs of water above the firmament and that, at the command of God these were periodically released as rain. Amos gave a more accurate description of the natural process, when he said that Jehovah called the waters of the sea (i.e. by evaporation) and poured them out over the face of the earth (i.e. as rain).

The mighty One, in whose hand are heaven and earth, by whom they were created and by whom they are still maintained, named Himself as Jehovah, the eternally existing One. With Him there is neither beginning or ending. All is comprehended in Him.

LIKE OTHER NATIONS

Are you not like the sons of the Ethiopians to me, O people of Israel? says Jehovah. Did I not bring up Israel from the land of Egypt? And the Philistines from Caphtor, and the Syrians from Kir? (9 : 7).

Israel had rejected the message of Jehovah through Amos and had unrepentantly continued their evil practices. They lived as though God did not exist and they would never have to acount to Him for the manner in which they had lived. Virtually they placed themselves on the same level as their heathen neighbours, who had no relationship with Jehovah. It was, therefore, only logical that God should accept their assessment of the situation and treat them as though they were no more to Him than any other nation. They had boasted of being the elect nation, but election was of no value to those who were idolatrous in practice and rebellious in heart.

The most remote people they knew were the Cushites or Ethiopians, who inhabited Nubia, and whom they despised for their dark colour, although Moses's wife was a Cushite (Num. 12: 1). They occasionally employed Cushites as servants or slaves (Jer. 38 : 7), but had no respect for the nation. Yet God declared that degenerate Israel was no more to Him than the Cushites.

Israel often referred to their deliverance from Egypt as being due primarily to the power of Jehovah. Very well. If He brought up Israel from the land of Egypt, and gave them the land of Canaan for their possession, had He not similarly directed the migrations of other nations? He had, for example, brought the Philistines from Caphtor or Crete (Jer. 47: 4). The Septuagint substitutes Cappadocia for Caphtor, which would make the original Philistine home Asia Minor, but Crete is the more probable origin. It was His hand, moreover, that directed the movement of the Aramæans (or Syrians) from Kir in Mesopotamia. These two races had been the consistent foes of Israel and it was all the more humiliating, therefore, to be informed that Jehovah had motivated their migrations equally with that of Israel.

He made it perfectly clear that He was not the private and exclusive property of Israel and that He was concerned with all nations of the world—a lesson which the apostle Paul had to teach again in New Testament days (Rom. 3 : 20). Since the people of Israel treated in such a cavalier fashion their relationship with Him and the special privileges He had bestowed upon them, it was only meet that they should be reminded that there were others of His creatures in whom He was also interested.

Von Rad (*ibid,* p. 133), commenting on the references made by Amos to political matters, says, "they leave us amazed at the clearsightedness of his observations of history. How accurate he was when he connected the so-called 'Aramæan migration' with the entirely different movement of the 'sea-peoples'

(Am. 9 : 7)! Both thrusts occurred at nearly the same time (i.e. *circa* 1200 B.C.), and political conditions in Palestine were fundamentally affected by them for long afterwards." His accuracy, of course, extends to far more than political matters and covers *inter alia* history and geography as well.

THE DISPERSION

Behold the eyes of Adonai Jehovah are upon the sinful kingdom, and I will destroy it from off the face of the earth; except that I will not utterly destroy the house of Jacob, says Jehovah. For, lo, I will command and I will shake the house of Israel to and fro among all the nations as one shakes with a sieve, yet not the least pebble shall fall upon the earth. All the sinners of my people shall die by the sword, who say, Evil shall not overtake us or meet us (9 : 8-10).

Lest there should be any dubiety, God stated that Israel (like any other nation) was under His surveillance, but His eyes, as He had stated previously (v. 4) were against them. They were a sinful kingdom and His intention was to destroy it from off the face of the earth. Were His promises and covenants to be rendered nugatory then? No: for, as ever through the history of this people there has been preserved a remnant, so now His purpose was to save some. "I will not utterly destroy the house of Jacob."

His command was that Israel should be sieved like grain, shaken to and fro among the nations. "The sieve (mentioned only here in the O.T.)," writes Mays (*ibid*, p. 161), "is one of a large mesh used to separate trash from grain. In threshing, wheat was first beaten or shredded on the threshing floor to separate the grains from stalk and husk, then winnowed to allow the light chaff to blow to one side. The remaining grain would contain trash and small stones. The large mesh sieve was used to catch the larger debris and let the smaller grains fall through." He would shake Israel so violently that only the solid grains would be preserved: all the trash would be lost. For centuries the work has continued and is still continuing until the wise purpose of the Eternal has been accomplished.

Yet he said emphatically that all the sinners of His people would be slain by the sword. The immediate reference, of course, was to the Assyrian invasion, but there has been more than one fulfilment of the statement and there may yet be others. Those immediately under sentence, however, were men who buoyed themselves up with the misplaced confidence that no evil could possibly overtake them or affect their lives. The false security in which they placed their reliance was to be the very cause of their destruction.

Human nature does not change. How many there are who dogmatically claim to be completely immune from trouble because they belong to Christ! God is more concerned with life and conduct than with pious professions and confident claims.

DAVID'S TABERNACLE

In that day I will raise up the tabernacle of David that is fallen, and repair its breaches, and I will raise up its ruins and rebuild it as in days of old: that they may possess the remnant of Edom and of all the nations who are called by my name, says Jehovah who does this (9 : 11, 12).

The covenant into which God entered with David centuries earlier provided that David's prosperity would never be completely exterminated, his dynasty would be permanent, and his political kingdom of Israel would continue for ever (2 Sam. 7 : 12-16; 1 Chron. 17 : 11-14; 22 : 9, 10). This did not imply that there would be an unbroken succession of kings of David's line (Psa. 89 : 38-45), but the fulfilment of the promise required that a descendant of the royal house shall sit on the throne (Jer. 33 : 17-21). With the conquest of Israel by the Assyrians and of Judah by the Babylonians and the forcible evacuation of the people from their own countries, the fulfilment of the covenant must have seemed remote.

Amos's prophecy, however, specifically predicted that "in that day", God would raise up the fallen tabernacle, or booth, of David and repair its breaches, raise up its ruins and rebuild it as in days of old. The significance was perfectly clear. The kingdom was to fall but, at some future date, God would raise it again and restore it to its former glory. The promise, of course, went beyond Israel and indicated that the united kindom of Israel and Judah would be restored. That has not yet occurred and the use of the term "days of old" implied that a long period would elapse between the fall and rising again.

At the Jerusalem council to discuss the question of circumcision in relation to Gentile converts, James referred to Peter's report that God had visited the Gentiles to take out of them a people for His name, and then declared that this was in agreement with the Old Testament prophecy. Quoting mainly from the Septuagint of Amos 9 : 11, 12, he rendered it, "After this I will return, and I will rebuild the tabernacle of David which is fallen; and I will rebuild its ruins and set it up; that the residue of men might seek after the Lord, and all the nations upon whom my name is called, says the Lord, who does these things" (Acts 15 : 16, 17). The wording employed by James differed considerably from the Massoretic text.

In his *Commentary on the Book of Acts* (p. 310), F. F. Bruce says, "The primary sense of the Massoretic text is that the fortunes of the fallen house of David will be restored and it will rule over all the territory which had been included in David's empire." This is obviously the significance, but then he continues, "James's application of the prophecy finds the fulfilment of the first part (the rebuilding of the tabernacle of David) in the resurrection and exaltation of Christ, the Son of David, and the reconstitution of His disciples as 'the new Israel', and the fulfilment of the second part in the presence of believing Gentiles as well as believing Jews in the church." W. J. Grier takes the same line in *The Momentous Event* (p. 35) when he says, "James declares that this rebuilding of the tabernacle of David is now taking place in God's visiting the Gentiles to take out of them a people for His name. By the ingathering of the Gentiles, God is repairing the broken-down condition of the Old Testament church."

A re-reading of James's words will make it quite clear, however, that his purpose in citing Amos 9 : 11, 12 was the sanctioning of the reception of Gentiles without circumcision. He did not imply (and nor does any other N.T. writer) that the church is to be identified with the tabernacle of David. As one writer pertinently remarks, this suggestion is quite "foreign and opposed to Scripture. It is only the allegorical habit of the fathers which invented the fiction that Zion or Jerusalem, that Judah or Israel, means the church." God has certainly not yet raised up the fallen tabernacle.

The plain meaning of the verses is that, after the calling out of the Gentiles, God will turn to David's house and renew its fortunes and restore the kingdom to the royal house. It is significant that Amos stated, "I will rebuild it as in the days of old." Patently the blessings resulting from the future restoration will be consistent with the promise of the past. They will be national and terrestrial and will have nothing to do with the church.

The prophecy also pledged that, when the dilapidated building is re-erected and repaired, when the kingdom has been restored and a scion of David sits upon the throne, then Israel will possess "the remnant of Edom and of all the nations who are called by" the name of Jehovah. At the very least, this assures the restoration of all the territory which originally formed part of David's kingdom. Driver considers that the nations called by God's name are those subjugated by David under God and which consequently were under the dominion of Jehovah.

So that, despite the outpouring of judgment upon the guilty nation, their dispersion and suffering, Amos plainly declared that there yet remained a glorious future for Israel. This was confirmed in the closing verses of his book.

MILLENNIAL BLESSINGS

Behold, the days are coming, says Jehovah, when the ploughman shall overtake the reaper, and the treader of grapes him who sows the seed: and the mountains shall drip with sweet wine, and all the hills shall flow into it. And I will reverse the captivity of my people of Israel, and they shall rebuild the ruined cities and inhabit them; and they shall plant vineyards and drink their wine; they shall also make gardens and eat their fruit. I will plant them in their own land, and they shall never again be plucked up out of their land which I have given them, says Jehovah your Elohim (9 : 13-15).

Using the eschatological formula employed previously by Amos, Jehovah looked on to the glorious millennial age and declared that the days were coming when there would be a period of unparalleled fertility in the land. Growth would be so rapid that the reaper would be at work almost immediately after the ploughman had broken up the ground. Normally ploughing commenced after the October rains. Sowing followed and the barley and wheat were ready for harvesting in April and May, and the grapes were gathered in August and September.

In the hyperbolical description given in Amos, however, as soon as the ground had been broken up and the seed sown, the harvest was ripe; and as soon as the grapes were gathered and trodden down in the winepress, the time had arrived for again sowing the seed. Moreover, the vines would be so loaded with grapes that the mountain slopes on which they were grown would drip and flow with sweet wine, and the hillsides would contribute their tributaries to the flow.

Israel would be restored to her land, never again to be removed therefrom. The people would rebuild the old ruined cities and then live in them. They would plant vineyards and make gardens, and drink the wine produced from the vineyards and eat the fruit grown in the gardens. No interference would be suffered in that day. It was to be one of peace and prosperity. Since God would plant the people in their land, nothing whatsoever could disturb them. They would never again be removed.

The picture is one of undeserved blessing. Amos makes no reference to the repentance and confession which will occur when Israel sees her Messiah, the author of all her blessings. Amos merely foretells the blessings which will result from His appearance. The agelong covenant will be fully implemented and the implication is presumably that the nation will turn in penitence and contrition to the One they rejected. With all their failures and shortcomings, they are still God's people and will be blessed by Him.

BIBLIOGRAPHY

D. C. BAER:	*The Message of the Prophets*, Pulpit Digest, Great Neck, 1940.
R. S. CRIPPS:	*A Critical and Exegetical Commentary on the Book of Amos*, S.P.C.K., London, 1955.
S. R. DRIVER:	*The Books of Joel and Amos*, Cambridge University Press, Cambridge, 1942.
E. A. EDGHILL:	*The Book of Amos*, Methuen & Co. Ltd., London, 1926.
F. C. EISELEN:	*The Minor Prophets*, Eaton & Mains, New York, 1907. *The Prophetic Books of the Old Testament*, Methodist Book Concern, New York, 1923.
H. L. ELLISON:	*The Prophets of Israel*, Paternoster Press, Exeter, 1969.
F. W. FARRAR:	*The Minor Prophets*, Fleming H. Revell Co., New York, n.d.
C. L. FEINBERG:	*Joel, Amos and Obadiah*, American Board of Missions to the Jews, New York, 1948.
D. D. GARLAND:	*Amos: A Study Guide*, Zondervan Publishing Co., Grand Rapids, 1973.
R. M. GWYNNE:	*The Book of Amos*, Cambridge University Press, Cambridge, 1927.
H. HAILEY:	*A Commentary on the Minor Prophets*, Baker Book House, Grand Rapids, 1972.
E. HAMMERHAIMB:	*The Book of Amos*, Schockson Books, New York, 1970.
W. R. HARPER:	*A Critical and Exegetical Comentary on Amos and Hosea*, T. & T. Clark, Edinburgh, 1953.

R. L. HONEYCUTT:	*Amos and His Message,* Broadman Press, Nashville, 1963.
R. F. HORTON:	*The Minor Prophets,* T.C. & E.C. Jack Edinburgh, 1906.
W. S. HOTTEL:	*Hosea—Malahi,* Union Gospel Press, Cleveland, n.d.
H. A. IRONSIDE:	*The Minor Prophets,* Loizeaux Bros. Inc., Neptune, n.d.
A. S. KAPELRUD:	*Central Issues in Amos,* Oslo University Press, Oslo, 1961.
C. F. KEIL:	*The Twelve Minor Prophets,* Wm. B. Eerdmans Publishing Co., Grand Rapids, 1961.
P. H. KELLEY:	*Amos: Prophet of Social Justice,* Baker Book House, Grand Rapids, 1972.
W. KELLY:	*Lectures Introductory to the Study of the Minor Prophets,* W. H. Broom & Rouse, London, 1897.
C. KUHL:	*The Prophets of Israel,* Oliver and Boyd Ltd., Edinburgh, 1960.
T. LAETSCH:	*The Minor Prophets,* Concordia Publishing Co., St. Louis, 1956.
J. P. LANGE:	*The Minor Prophets,* Zondervan Publishing House, Grand Rapids, n.d.
W. LUTHI:	*In the Time of the Earthquake,* Hodder & Stoughton Ltd., London, 1940.
J. E. MCFADYEN:	*A Cry for Justice: A Study in Amos,* Charles Scribners' Sons, New York, 1912.
H. MCKEATING:	*The Books of Amos, Hosea and Micah,* Cambridge University Press, Cambridge, 1971.
J. MARSH:	*Amos and Micah,* S.C.M. Press Ltd., London, 1959.

J. L. MAYS:	*Amos*, S.C.M. Press Ltd., London, 1969.
H. G. MITCHELL:	*Amos: An Essay in Exegesis*, Houghton, Mifflin & Co., Boston, 1900.
E. B. PUSEY:	*The Minor Prophets*, Baker Book House, Grand Rapids, 1970.
G. L. ROBINSON:	*Twelve Minor Prophets*, Baker Book House, Grand Rapids, 1952.
O. SCHMOLLER:	*Amos* in Lange's Commentary—see above.
G. A. SMITH:	*The Book of the Twelve Prophets*, Hodder & Stoughton Ltd., London, 1905.
R. L. SMITH:	*Amos* in *The Broadman Bible Commentary*, Marshall, Morgan & Scott Ltd., London, 1973.
N. H. SNAITH:	*The Book of Amos*, Epworth Press, London, 1956.
T. H. SUTCLIFFE:	*The Book of Amos*, S.P.C.K., London, 1939.
J. B. TAYLOR:	*The Minor Prophets*, Scripture Union, London, 1970.
B. THOROGOOD:	*A Guide to the Book of Amos*, S.P.C.K., London, 1971.
J. M. WARD:	*Amos and Isaiah*, Abingdon Press, Nashville, 1969.
J. D. W. WATTS:	*Studying the Book of Amos*, Broadman Press, Nashville, 1966.
	Vision and Prophecy in Amos, Wm. B. Eerdmans Publishing Co., Grand Rapids, 1958.
R. E. WOLFE:	*Meet Amos and Hosea*, Harper & Bros., New York, 1945.
H. W. WOLFF:	*Amos the Prophet*, Fortress Press, Philadelphia, 1973.
E. J. YOUNG:	*My Servants the Prophets*, Wm. B. Eerdmans Publishing Co., Grand Rapids, 1952.

BOOKS BY DR. F. A. TATFORD

God's Programme of the Ages, £1.00 Chapters on all aspects of prophecy.

The Clock Strikes, 60p. A novel concerning the end times.

Five Minutes to Midnight, 35p. Topical events and their relation to the future.

Born to Burn, 60p. The fascinating story of a missionary tortured for years by Japanese.

Man Who Could Not Die, 25p. The thrilling story of a young Russian whom death repeatedly evaded.

Life Isn't All Honey, 35p. Many of the problems of life.

Festivals of Israel, 30p. The prophetic significance of the festivals.

Prophecy's Last Word, 50p. An exhaustive commentary on the Book of Revelation.

Climax of the Ages, 50p. A scholarly exposition of Daniel.

Prince of Darkness, 30p. A comprehensive study of Satan.

Prophet from the Euphrates, 40p. Balaam and his parables.

Prophet of Edom's Doom, 35p. An exposition of Obadiah.

Prophet of the Restoration, 35p. An exposition of Haggai.

Prophet of the Myrtle Grove, £1.25. An exposition of Zechariah.

Prophet of the Reformation, 40p. An exposition of Malachi.

Going into Europe, 5p. The Common Market and its significance.

Israel and Her Future, 5p. A clear and topical statement.

Resurrection, 5p. Scriptural and sound.

The Seventy Weeks, 5p. A *multum in parvo*.

Outline of Events, 5p. The prophetic future.

What Does the Future Hold? 2½p. A brief outline.

The Coming of Christ, 2½p. The Advent and the unconverted.

Is Life Worth Living. 2½p. The evangelic message.

Obtainable from:

PROPHETIC WITNESS PUBLISHING CO.,

Upperton House, The Avenue, Eastbourne,

Sussex, BN21 3YB.